John Austin Stevens

Proceedings at the Mass Meeting of Loyal Citizens, on Union Square, New-York,

15th day of July, 1862, under the auspices of the Chamber of commerce of the state of New York, the Common council of the city of New York

John Austin Stevens

Proceedings at the Mass Meeting of Loyal Citizens, on Union Square, New-York, 15th day of July, 1862, under the auspices of the Chamber of commerce of the state of New York, the Common council of the city of New York

ISBN/EAN: 9783337301538

Printed in Europe, USA, Canada, Australia, Japan

Cover: Foto ©ninafisch / pixelio.de

More available books at **www.hansebooks.com**

PROCEEDINGS

AT THE

Mass Meeting of Loyal Citizens,

ON

UNION SQUARE, NEW-YORK,

15th DAY OF JULY, 1862,

UNDER THE AUSPICES OF

THE CHAMBER OF COMMERCE OF THE STATE OF NEW-YORK, THE UNION DEFENCE COMMITTEE OF THE CITIZENS OF NEW-YORK, THE COMMON COUNCIL OF THE CITY OF NEW-YORK,

AND OTHER COMMITTEES

OF

LOYAL CITIZENS.

LETTERS AND SPEECHES.

PUBLISHED BY ORDER OF THE COMMITTEE OF ARRANGEMENTS UNDER THE SUPERVISION OF

JOHN AUSTIN STEVENS, Jr., *Secretary.*

NEW-YORK:
GEORGE F. NESBITT & CO., PRINTERS,
CORNER OF PEARL AND PINE STS.

1862.

PRELIMINARY PROCEEDINGS.

ORGANIZATION OF COMMITTEES.

CHAMBER OF COMMERCE OF THE STATE OF NEW-YORK,
NEW-YORK, *July* 3d, 1862.

At a meeting of the Chamber of Commerce, held this day, the President in the chair, the following Preamble and Resolutions were unanimously adopted:—

On the 19th day of April, 1861, the Chamber of Commerce of the State of New-York declared its sentiments in regard to the duty of loyal citizens of the United States to sustain the Government in its efforts to suppress a wicked and injurious rebellion, then but recently commenced.

In accordance with the sentiments at that time expressed, and in the discharge of the like obligations of duty to the country, this Chamber does hereby

RESOLVE—

First. That it will continue to sustain, by its influence with the commercial community and to the fullest extent of its means, the National Government in a vigorous and determined effort to maintain the integrity of the Union, and effectually to put down rebellion.

Second. That in the recent appeal made by the President to the loyalty of the country for additional military forces, the Chamber recognizes the patriotism and energy which should insure confidence in his fidelity to the Constitution, and in his determination to preserve the National honor.

Third. That this Chamber will cordially unite with other bodies of loyal citizens in any measures calculated to give efficiency to the military and naval power of the Government, and to preserve and maintain the character of this community for patriotism and loyal devotion to the Union.

Further. That a Committee of thirteen members be appointed by the chair to consider and recommend to the Chamber, such measures as they may deem advisable, to give practical effect to this expression of the sentiments of the Chamber.

The President named as such Committee:

GEORGE OPDYKE, *Chairman.*

JOHN A. STEVENS, CHARLES H. MARSHALL,
A. A. LOW, S. D. BABCOCK,
PROSPER M. WETMORE, GEORGE W. BLUNT,
DENNING DUER, ROBT. B. MINTURN,
WILLIAM E. DODGE, JONATHAN STURGES,
CHRISTOPHER R. ROBERT, ROYAL PHELPS.

A true extract from the Records of the Chamber.

JOHN AUSTIN STEVENS, Jr.,
Secretary.

A copy of the Preamble and Resolutions was, by direction of the President of the Chamber, engrossed and forwarded to the President of the United States.

CHAMBER OF COMMERCE OF THE STATE OF NEW-YORK,
NEW-YORK, *July* 5*th*, 1862.

To the President of the United States:

SIR,—I have the honor to present a copy of Preamble and Resolutions unanimously adopted by this Chamber at their general meeting this day.

The Chamber show the will to meet with cheerfulness all present sacrifices, and the determination to aid the Government to the extent of their ability in prompt and vigorous prosecution of the war, until the national authority is re-established and the integrity of the Union restored.

With great respect, your obedient servant,

JOHN AUSTIN STEVENS, Jr.,
Secretary of the Chamber of Commerce.

On the 5th July, the Committee of Thirteen, appointed by the Chamber, met and addressed invitations to the Union Defence Committee of the citizens of New-York and the Common Council of the city of New-York, inviting their co-operation.

CHAMBER OF COMMERCE ROOMS,
NEW-YORK, *July* 5*th*, 1862.

To the Union Defence Committee of the Citizens of New-York:

GENTLEMEN,—I have the honor to communicate the following resolution, unanimously passed this day by a Committee appointed on the part of the Chamber to take into consideration the present state of our national affairs:

Resolved, That a committee of five be appointed to meet a similar committee from the Union Defence Committee, and committees from other bodies of loyal citizens, to unite upon the proper measures to sustain the National Government in crushing out this rebellion, with power to call this committee together to receive their report.

Under this resolution the following gentlemen were appointed on the part of the Chamber of Commerce:

Hon. GEORGE OPDYKE, *Chm'n*,
C. R. ROBERT,
JONATHAN STURGES,
DENNING DUER,
JOHN A. STEVENS.

With great respect. your obedient servant,

JOHN AUSTIN STEVENS, Jr.,
Secretary.

UNION DEFENCE COMMITTEE OF THE CITIZENS OF NEW-YORK, }
NEW-YORK, *July 8th*, 1862. }

John Austin Stevens, Jr., Esq., Secretary of the Chamber of Commerce:

SIR,—I am instructed to acknowledge your communication of this day, inviting a deputation from this body to confer with a committee of the Chamber of Commerce in relation to the public affairs of the country.

This committee will cheerfully unite with the Chamber in the furtherance of any measures calculated to promote the public welfare; and I am accordingly instructed to transmit to you the following names composing a committee of conference:

Messrs. HAMILTON FISH,
A. T. STEWART,
R. M. BLATCHFORD,
P. M. WETMORE.
A. C. RICHARDS,
R. A. WITTHAUS,
SAMUEL SLOAN,

I am, respectfully, your obedient servant,

PROSPER M. WETMORE,
Secretary pro tem.

UNION DEFENCE COMMITTEE, }
NEW-YORK, *July 12th*, 1862. }

SIR:

In accordance with the expressed desire of the Convention of Committees appointed to call a public meeting of the citizens of New-York, I am instructed to inform you that the action in question received the sanction of all the members of this committee present at the meeting of the 8th inst., viz.:

HAMILTON FISH, *Chairman*,
SIMEON DRAPER,
SAMUEL SLOAN,
WM. E. DODGE,
Hon. GEO. OPDYKE,
ROBT. T. HAWS,
ISAAC BELL.
R. M. BLATCHFORD,
M. H. GRINNELL,
R. H. MCCURDY,
R. A. WITTHAUS,
W. F. HAVEMEYER,
A. C. RICHARDS,
P. M. WETMORE.

I am, respectfully, your obedient servant,

PROSPER M. WETMORE,
Secretary pro tem.

JOHN AUSTIN STEVENS, Jr., Esq., *Secretary Joint Convention.*

PROCEEDINGS OF BOARD OF ALDERMEN.

The following communication was received from His Honor the Mayor, transmitting a communication from the Chamber of Commerce, relative to the state of our national affairs:—

MAYOR'S OFFICE, NEW-YORK,
July 7th, 1862.

To the Honorable the Common Council:

GENTLEMEN,—The events of the last fortnight appear to call for a renewed expression of our devotion to our country, and of our unfaltering determination to sustain the Government in its efforts to suppress the rebellion. After an almost uninterrupted series of victories for half a year, we have at last met with two reverses—one at Charleston and the other before Richmond—which, though indecisive and temporary, do yet disappoint our confident expectations, and tend to prolong the war, supposed by some to be well-nigh ended. Upon such a disappointment, it seems fitting that we, as the official organ of the most populous and opulent city of the Republic, should repeat the declaration of unwavering constancy, which neither victory nor defeat can change, and our unalterable resolution to stand by the Government in maintaining the supremacy of the Constitution and the integrity of the country, at all hazards, and at every necessary sacrifice of life and treasure.

In the presence of the great conflict in which the country is engaged, we will forget all past differences of party or opinion—for all party considerations sink into insignificance in the presence of danger to the Government itself: we will summon every loyal citizen to join us in supporting the Government, and to aid us by his services and counsel; we will give a generous confidence to the President and all whom, in the exercise of his just authority, he thinks proper to place in positions under him; and while we must exercise the privilege of freemen, to criticise public men, and exact from them fidelity to their trusts, vigor and promptitude in action, and such a comprehensive and well-considered policy, as to adapt the means to the end—availing, for this purpose, of all the instrumentalities that the usages of civilized warfare will justify—we will declare to them that our lives and fortunes are at the service of our country, and that we ask only to be informed how much is needed, and to be assured that what we give shall be faithfully and wisely applied to that service.

It is one of the uses of national reverses that they serve to winnow the disloyal from the loyal. Now is the time to know who is true and who is false. The country never needed the services of traitors, and now less than ever. But she does need the services of all her loyal children, that she may not only overthrow this gigantic but causeless rebellion against her authority but may repel, with becoming spirit, the first approach to that foreign intervention in her affairs which is at times obscurely threatened, and which we cannot admit for one instant without national disgrace. Let us, then, seek out, discover, and bring to punishment every disloyal person; and let us call on all the loyal to stand together, and to speak and act as one man, for the safety and honor of their country. If we had never had a victory: if, from the beginning of the war till now, a series of uninterrupted disasters had fallen upon our armies, we could not even then have compromised with revolt, or submitted to dismemberment, without the basest pusillanimity. But our arms have been, for the most part, victorious; the area of the rebellion has been gradually contracted by the advances of the armies of the Union; the great rivers of the West have been opened; all but four of the seaports on the whole coast, from Cape Henry to the Rio Grande, have been retaken and restored to the Union. The Federal authority has been re-established over many fortresses and cities, where a year ago it was contemned, and we are gradually winning them all back by the irresistible force of our arms. Our country has, therefore, no cause of discouragement, but every reason to hope, and every motive to persevere.

Considering these things, I suggest respectfully to your Honorable Bodies, the propriety of passing resolutions, pledging the people of this Metropolis to the support of the Government in the prosecution of the war and the maintenance of the national honor; and that you authorize your Joint Committee on National Affairs to unite with the Committee of the Chamber of Commerce, and other committees acting with them, in calling a public meeting of citizens of all parties, to express, without reference to any party question whatever, their undiminished confidence in the justice of our cause, their inflexible purpose to maintain it to the end, and to proffer to the Government all the aid it may need, to the extent of all our resources.

Since writing the above, I have received the accompanying resolution of the Chamber of Commerce, on the same subject, with a request that it be transmitted to your Honorable Body.

GEORGE OPDYKE,

Mayor.

CHAMBER OF COMMERCE OF THE STATE OF NEW-YORK, } NEW-YORK, *July 5th,* 1862.

To the Honorable the Common Council of the City of New-York:

I have the honor to communicate to your Honorable Body, the following resolution, passed unanimously this day, by a committee appointed on the part of the Chamber of Commerce, to take into consideration the state of national affairs:

Resolved, That a committee of five be appointed, to meet a similar committee from the Union Defence Committee, and committees from other bodies of loyal citizens, to unite upon the proper measures to sustain the National Government, in crushing out this rebellion, with power to call this Committee together to receive their report.

Under this resolution, the following gentlemen were appointed on the part of the Chamber of Commerce:

Hon. GEORGE OPDYKE,   DENNING DUER,
C. R. ROBERT,   JOHN A. STEVENS,
JONATHAN STURGES.

With respect, your obedient servant,

JOHN AUSTIN STEVENS, Jr.,

Secretary.

Alderman DAYTON moved that the communication from his Honor the Mayor be referred to the Joint Committee on National Affairs, and that the Committee on National Affairs be authorized and directed to co-operate with the Committee of the Chamber of Commerce, in the manner recommended by his Honor the Mayor in his communication.

The whole subject was referred to Committee on National Affairs.

Same documents sent to Board of Councilmen, and thereupon Councilman ORTON moved that the communication be received and referred to the Committee on National Affairs, with power to confer with any other committees relative to the state of the Union, if in their judgment advisable.

Which was carried.

The Joint committee on National Affairs appointed as a sub-committee to confer with the other committees the following:

COUNCILMAN WM. ORTON, *Chairman.*

Ald. PETER MITCHELL,   Councilman WM. II. GEDNEY.
" HENRY SMITH,   Ald. IRA A. ALLEN.

This committee attended, and chose Ald. MITCHELL to represent them on the Committee on Resolutions.

MEETING OF CONVENTION OF COMMITTEES.

The joint Committees of the Chamber of Commerce, the Union Defence Committee and the Common Council, met on Wednesday, the 9th of July. A Committee of five on the part of a body of citizens, who met at the Mayor's office, July 7th, consisting of—

    JUDGE JAMES W. WHITE, *Chairman,*
  Dr. FRANCIS LIEBER,   GEO. D. PHELPS,
  DAVID DUDLEY FIELD,   ISAAC SHERMAN,

appeared, and was requested to take part in the proceedings: as was also a Committee of five, on the part of a body of citizens who met at Fifth Avenue Hotel:

    ROBERT H. McCURDY, *Chairman,*
  CHARLES GOULD,   MORRIS KETCHUM,
  WILLIAM CURTIS NOYES,   NATHANIEL HAYDEN.

A sub-committee was appointed to draft and prepare an Address and a series of Resolutions, to be submitted for ratification to a public meeting, to be called at an early day.

An Address and Resolutions were submitted on the 10th of July, and unanimously adopted.

The Committee of Thirteen appointed by the Chamber of Commerce, met on the same day, and unanimously ratified the action of their sub-committee.

The Chamber of Commerce met on the same day, to receive the report of the Committee of Thirteen, which was unanimously accepted, and the Committee continued, with power to carry out the objects proposed.

A true abstract of the proceedings of the Chamber of Commerce and of joint Convention.

                JOHN AUSTIN STEVENS, Jr.,
      Secretary of Chamber of Commerce and of Joint Convention.

INVITATION TO THE PRESIDENT OF THE UNITED STATES.

In accordance with a resolution of the Committee of Arrangements, a sub-committee consisting of Hon. George Opdyke, J. W. White, Samuel Sloan, Denning Duer, and R. H. McCurdy, was appointed to visit Washington, and to request the President of the United States to be present at the meeting. Two of the Committee being unexpectedly prevented by other pressing engagements from fulfilling the commission, F. S. Winston, though not a member of the Committee, was subsequently added. A copy of the Address and Resolutions was handsomely engrossed and placed in the hands of the Chairman, for delivery to the President; and the following letter was also addressed, to serve as the credentials of the Committee.

ROOMS OF THE CHAMBER OF COMMERCE OF THE STATE OF NEW-YORK, }
NEW-YORK, *July* 10*th*, 1862. }

To the President of the United States:

SIR,—I have the honor to inform you that at a Convention, held this day, of Committees severally appointed by the Chamber of Commerce of the State of New-York, the Union Defence Committee, the Common Council of the city, and other bodies of loyal citizens, it was unanimously

Resolved, To hold a public meeting of the citizens of New-York, in favor of supporting the government in the prosecution of the war, and the suppression of the rebellion; to express, without reference to any party question whatever, their undiminished confidence in the justice of our cause, and their inflexible purpose to maintain it to the end, and to proffer to the Government all the aid it may need, to the extent of all their resources.

A Committee of Arrangements was appointed, to take all measures to render the meeting as effective as the occasion for it demands, by whose direction, and in whose behalf, Messrs. J. W. White, R. H. McCurdy, and F. S. Winston, visit the capital to earnestly invite the presence of the President of the United States at the proposed meeting, believing that such course will arouse the enthusiasm of this city, of this State, and of the whole country, in this imminent crisis of the national destiny.

By order of the Committee of Arrangements,

GEORGE OPDYKE,	HENRY SMITH,
DENNING DUER,	GEORGE D. PHELPS,
JONATHAN STURGES,	J. W. WHITE,
SAMUEL SLOAN,	CHARLES GOULD.
P. M. WETMORE,	ROBERT H. MCCURDY.
PETER MITCHELL,	

A true extract from the Minutes.

Respectfully, your most obedient servant,

JOHN AUSTIN STEVENS, Jr.,
Secretary of Convention, and of Committee of Arrangements.

WASHINGTON, *July* 12*th*, 1862.

To the President:

SIR,—The undersigned have been appointed by a Convention of Committees, from the Common Council, the Chamber of Commerce, the Union Defence Committee, and other loyal bodies in the city of New-York, to proceed to this city and present to you the invitation of the Convention, to attend a mass meeting of the citizens of New-York, to be convened on Tuesday, 15th instant, for the purpose of declaring their continued inflexible determination to support the Government at all hazards, and in every measure necessary for the suppression of the existing rebellion, "and, to that end, to proffer to the Government all the aid in their power, to the extent of all their resources."

Presenting to you, sir, this invitation, which we have been commissioned to deliver, we beg leave respectfully to add, that we have been charged by the Convention to say, that, in their judgment, nothing could be more gratifying to the people of New-York, or would tend more to invigorate the patriotism which animates every loyal heart, than to meet their Chief Magistrate thus in General Council in this momentous crisis of our national destiny.

The Convention are aware that the act to which they thus invite the President of the United States—to attend a mass meeting of citizens assembled to consider important national questions—is one not in accordance with any previous usage or precedent: but when they remember that the occasion is one without a precedent in the past, and which they trust in God will be without anything like it in the future—a struggle with a rebellion which, in the history of the world, has no parallel, for its causelessness, its magnitude, and its monstrous wickedness as a crime against the whole human race, the Convention hope that you may be able to lay aside for a day other important public duties, and meet your loyal fellow-citizens at the time and in the manner suggested.

We are, sir, with the greatest respect and consideration,

Your obedient servants,

JAMES W. WHITE,
ROBERT H. MCCURDY, } *Committee.*
FREDERICK S. WINSTON,

To ABRAHAM LINCOLN, *President of the United States.*

REPLY OF THE PRESIDENT OF THE UNITED STATES.

EXECUTIVE MANSION, }
WASHINGTON, *July* 14*th*, 1862. }

Messrs. James W. White, Robert H. McCurdy, and F. H. Winston, Committee:

GENTLEMEN.—Your letter conveying to me the invitation of several loyal and patriotic bodies in New-York to attend a mass meeting in that city, on Tuesday, the 15th inst., is received. While it would be very agreeable to me to thus meet the friends of the country, I am sure I could add nothing to the purpose or the wisdom with which they will perform their duty; and the near adjournment of Congress makes it indispensable for me to remain here. Thanking you and those you represent for this invitation, and the kind terms in which you have communicated it,

I remain, your obedient servant,

A. LINCOLN.

INVITATION TO CORPORATIONS, ASSOCIATIONS AND SOCIETIES TO ATTEND THE MEETING OF LOYAL CITIZENS.

NEW-YORK, *July* 11*th*, 1862.

SIR:

At a Convention of Committees, severally appointed by the Common Council of this City; by the Chamber of Commerce of the State of New-York ; by the Union Defence Committee ; and by bodies of Loyal Citizens of this city, it was resolved to hold, on Tuesday, the 15th instant, a Mass Meeting of all parties who are in favor of supporting the Government in the prosecution of the war and suppressing the rebellion ; and to express, without reference to any party question whatever, their undiminished confidence in the justice of the cause, and their inflexible determination to sustain it ; and to that end to proffer to the Government their aid to the extent of all their resources.

In accordance with this purpose, the undersigned were appointed by the Convention a Committee to invite the attendance of all Associations, Corporations, and Societies.

In performance of this duty, we request that you will issue a call to the members of your Association, and convene them on the afternoon of Tuesday, to proceed to the Square, where accommodations will be provided, and places on the Stands be reserved for your officers.

JAMES W. WHITE,
GEO. OPDYKE,
SAMUEL SLOAN,
PROSPER M. WETMORE,
DENNING DUER,
CHARLES GOULD,
} *Select Committee.*

JOHN AUSTIN STEVENS, Jr., *Secretary of Convention.*

CALL FOR THE MEETING OF LOYAL CITIZENS.

The citizens of New-York, of all parties, who are for supporting the Government in the prosecution of the war and the suppression of the rebellion, are requested to meet on Union Square, on Tuesday afternoon next, 15th inst., at 4 o'clock, to express, without reference to any party question whatever, their undiminished confidence in the justice of our cause, and their inflexible purpose to maintain it to the end, and to proffer to the Government all the aid it may need to the extent of all their resources.

NEW-YORK, *July 10th*, 1862.

Committee of the Chamber of Commerce.

GEORGE OPDYKE, *Chairman*,
CHARLES H. MARSHALL,
S. D. BABCOCK,
G. W. BLUNT,
ROBERT B. MINTURN,
JONATHAN STURGES,
JOHN A. STEVENS,
A. A. LOW,
P. M. WETMORE,
DENNING DUER,
WILLIAM E. DODGE,
C. R. ROBERT,
ROYAL PHELPS.

Committee of the Union Defence Committee.

HAMILTON FISH, *Chairman*,
ROBERT T. HAWS,
SAMUEL SLOAN,
WILLIAM E. DODGE,
MOSES H. GRINNELL,
ISAAC BELL,
SIMEON DRAPER,
R. M. BLATCHFORD,
ALEX. T. STEWART,
R. A. WITTHAUS,
A. C. RICHARDS,
WILLIAM F. HAVEMEYER.

Committee on National Affairs of the Common Council of New-York.

WILLIAM ORTON, *Chairman*,
PETER MITCHELL,
WILLIAM H. GEDNEY,
CHARLES J. CHIPP,
JOHN HOGAN,
HENRY SMITH,
IRA A. ALLEN,
TERENCE FARLEY,
MORGAN JONES,
ALEX. H. KEECH.

A Committee of Citizens who met at the Mayor's Office.

JAMES W. WHITE, *Chairman*,
DAVID DUDLEY FIELD,
FRANCIS LIEBER,
GEORGE D. PHELPS,
ISAAC SHERMAN.

Committee of Citizens who met at Fifth Avenue Hotel.

ROBT. H. McCURDY, *Chairman*,
WILLIAM CURTIS NOYES,
CHARLES GOULD,
MORRIS KETCHUM,
NATHANIEL HAYDEN.

JOHN AUSTIN STEVENS, JR., *Secretary*.

REQUEST TO CITIZENS TO CLOSE PLACES OF BUSINESS.

The loyal citizens of every class and profession are respectfully and earnestly invited to attend the Grand Mass Meeting, to be held on Tuesday next, 15th inst., at four o'clock, on Union Square.

It is recommended that all places of business be closed at three o'clock, in order that those who desire to show their loyalty to the Government may be present.

By order of the Committee of Arrangements,

GEORGE OPDYKE,
Chairman.

JOHN AUSTIN STEVENS, Jr.,
Secretary.

The Committee of Arrangements, together with speakers and invited guests, met at the Everett House, to receive their several badges, and at precisely four o'clock, the procession was formed, and, preceded by the band and headed by the Mayor, moved toward the designated stands, amid salvos of artillery and accompanied by thousands of citizens.

OFFICERS.

STAND No. 1.

Under charge of Committee of Arrangements,

JONATHAN STURGES,   SAMUEL SLOAN

JOHN AUSTIN STEVENS, Jr.

President.

Hon. GEORGE OPDYKE, *Mayor of the city.*

Vice-Presidents.

JOHN T. HENRY,
JOHN J. PHELPS,
A. LOCKWOOD,
STEPHEN CAMBRELENG,
ELIJAH F. PURDY,
ROBERT T. HAWS,
EDWARDS PIERREPONT,
HIRAM BARNEY,
HORACE GREELEY,
RUFUS F. ANDREWS,
A. C. KINGSLAND,
JAMES BOORMAN,
DAVID DUDLEY FIELD,
SAMUEL R. BETTS,
NEHEMIAH KNIGHT,
WM. B. SHIPMAN,
CORNELIUS VANDERBILT,
EDWARD LEARNED,
SIMEON DRAPER,
CHARLES P. DALY,
ABRAM WAKEMAN,
CHARLES H. RUSSELL,
HENRY E. DAVIES,
PETER S. TITUS,
W. V. BRADY,
S. B. CHITTENDEN,
CHARLES BUTLER,
JOHN C. HAMILTON,
ROBERT MURRAY,
PAUL SPOFFORD,
GEORGE W. BROWN,
CHARLES BURKHALTER,
GREENE C. BRONSON,
SYDNEY MASON,
JOSEPH WALKER,
JAMES WHITING,

DANIEL F. TIEMANN,
MORRIS FRANKLIN,
CHAS. YATES,
CHAS. W. SANDFORD,
CHARLES LAMSON,
CHARLES J. CHIPP,
WILLIAM WATT,
A. DAVIDSON,
HENRY A. HEISER,
CHARLES H. MACY,
B. WESTERMANN,
FRED. WILLMAN,
N. ROSEMAN
BERNHARD COHEN,
HENRY BRUGGMAN,
JOSEPH LAWRENCE,
GEORGE T. ELLIOTT,
GEORGE F. THOMAE,
SAMUEL WETMORE,
WM. G. LAMBERT,
EDWIN HOYT,
WILLIAM OOTHOUT,
OLIVER S. STRONG,
ISAAC SHERMAN,
JEREMIAH BURNS,
ANDREW CARRIGAN,
JAMES A. HAMILTON,
GEORGE GREER,
RICHARD M. HOE,
FREDERICK H. WOLCOTT,
WALDEN PELL,
TEUNIS QUICK,
HYMAN MORANGE,
GEORGE B. BUTLER,
JAS. W. BEEKMAN,
ELI WHITE,

John Bailey,
J. M. Marsh,
Charles Nelson,
John J. Bradley,
Washington Smith,
Wm. H. Anthon,
David Belden,
Amos Robbins,
C. Y. Wemple,
John R. Brady,
John J Cisco,
E. Delafield Smith,
George Denison,
John P. Crosby,
Nathan Chandler,
J. S. Bosworth,
Charles G. Cornell,
James Moncrief,
Henry Brewster,
George Starr,
S. S. Wyckoff,
James Brooks,
George Bliss,
Edward S. Jaffray,
Thomas Lawrence,
Henry Hilton,
Clarence A. Seward,
George F Nesbitt,
George P. Putnam,
Erastus C. Benedict,
Thomas Stevenson,
Morgan Jones,
William F. Havemeyer,
Nathaniel Hayden,
Joseph Hoxie,
Eleazar Parmly,
Ira A. Allen,
Geo. F. Talman,
Benj. F. Manierre,
C. C. Pinckney,
Richard Busteed,
James Kelly,
Charles S. Spencer,
Levi Apgar,
William C. Wetmore,
Alex. H. Keech,
H. N. Willhelm,
R. Weil Van Genesback,
A. Windmuller,
Frederick Kuhne,
D. Lichtenstein,
M. Levin,
Andrus Whilman,
John Hayward,
B. W. Osborne,
Daniel Slate,
Daniel Wells,
P. Pfeiffer,

William W. Todd,
J. Pierrepont Morgan,
C. H. Marshall, Jr.,
Henry Vandewater,
M. D. Gale,
John Hayward,
C. H. Sand,
R. Vonder Heydt,
N. Wheeler,
J. B. Cornell,
Charles Steinway,
Ernest Predt,
Joseph Balestier,
Rudolph Dulon,
Otto Ernst,
David Miller,
M. S. Dunham,
Max Schaffer,
Charles Taylor,
Henry Seaman,
J. Penniman,
Latham Parker,
Nath. Worley,
Enoch Chamberlain,
Wm. H. Webb,
Henry S. Smith,
James Horn,
Philip Hamilton,
Warren Ward,
D. A. Wood,
Wade B. Worrall,
John H. Williams,
Frederick Reichfuss,
Eugene S. Ballin,
John Watson,
Benjamin Floyd,
Julius Brill,
William A. Kobbe,
Charles Schaffner,
Theodore J. Glaubensklee,
Leopold Bierwith,
Sigismund Kauffman,
Edward Byrnes,
Henry A. Casseleer,
Louis Naumann,
William Aufermann,
John C. Brant,
Isaac G. Ogden,
Oliver Holden,
Elias Howe, Jr.,
James K. Pell,
Nath'l W. Burtis,
A. Michelbacker,
Philip Frankenheimer,
A. Menzesheimer,
Charles Cludius,
William Scharfenberg,
William Tellinghause,

JOHN BROOKS,
JOHN E. GAVITT,
F. E. WELLINGTON,
SETH B. HUNT,
FRANK E. HOWE,
RICHARD BERRY,
JAMES GORDON BENNETT,
EZRA NYE,

ISAAC DAYTON,
ALEXANDER HAMILTON,
JOHN HOGAN,
ROBERT BAYARD,
SAMUEL HOTALING,
J. M. OLESEN,
SIGISMUND WATERMAN,
WILLIAM C. PRIME,

Secretaries.

JOHN AUSTIN STEVENS, Jr.,
JOHN M. WHITE,
FREDERICK STURGES,
WM. S. OPDYKE,
EDWARD A. WETMORE,
THEODORE ROOSEVELT,
BROCKHOLST CUTTING,
FRANCIS A. STOUT,
EDWARD KING,
WILLIAM F. CARY, Jr.,
JAMES W. UNDERHILL,
PETER MARIE,
CHARLES G. CLARK,
ALEXANDER BECKER,
JAMES E. MACRAN,
CRUGER OAKLEY,
WILLIAM J. TODD,
WASHINGTON MURRAY,
J. HOWARD WAINWRIGHT,
G. NORMAN LIEBER,
MURRAY HOFFMAN,
GEORGE McC. MILLER,
HENRY WINTHROP,
GEO. F. BETTS,
WM. F. SMITH,

SIDNEY WEBSTER,
R. FULTON CRARY,
LEWIS CARR,
JOSEPH H. CHOATE,
N. W. HOWELL,
JAMES COUPER LORD,
STUYVESANT LEROY,
ETHAN ALLEN,
ROBERT MORRIS VANDENHEUVEL,
JOHN MCCLAVE,
OSCAR SCHMIDT,
JOHN H. WHITE,
CHARLES H. TYLER,
SAMUEL W. TUBBS,
JOSEPH HOWARD, Jr.,
THEODORE TILTON,
JOHN J. WHITE,
WM. H. EVERETT,
WM. H. PEET.
JAS. H. FROTHINGHAM,
CHAS. E. STEVENS,
CLINTON RICE,
DAVID ROWLAND,
FLOYD SMITH,
B. H. HOWARD.

PROGRAMME OF PROCEEDINGS.

STAND No. 1.

SALUTES OF ARTILLERY, by the ANTHON LIGHT BATTERY, and by the WORKMEN employed by HENRY BREWSTER & CO.

1. GRAND MARCH by Mendelssohn, by Helmsmuller's Grand Band.
2. JONATHAN STURGES will call the meeting to order, read the CALL FOR THE MEETING, and conduct to the Chair, HON. GEORGE OPDYKE, Mayor of the City.
3. DENNING DUER will read the list of Vice-Presidents and Secretaries.
4. Hon. GEORGE OPDYKE, Chairman, will address the meeting.
5. DAVID DUDLEY FIELD will read the ADDRESS adopted by the Convention of Committees.
6. JOHN AUSTIN STEVENS, Jr., will read the RESOLUTIONS adopted by the Convention of Committees.
7. Song on our Country and our Flag, by FRANCIS LIEBER; sung by Grand Chorus with band accompaniment.
8. CHARLES KING will address the meeting.
9. WILLIAM ROSS WALLACE will read an Ode, composed for the occasion—"Keep Step to the Music of Union."
10. MUSIC—Star-Spangled Banner.
11. HIRAM WALBRIDGE will address the meeting.
12. MUSIC—Hail Columbia.
13. SENATOR SPINOLA will address the meeting.
14. MUSIC—Hail to the Chief.

Mr. JONATHAN STURGES called the meeting to order, read the call of the meeting, and conducted to the chair Hon. GEORGE OPDYKE, Mayor of the city, amid the cheers of the people.

In the absence of Mr. DENNING DUER, JOHN AUSTIN STEVENS, Jr., read the list of Vice-Presidents and Secretaries, which was adopted.

SPEECH OF THE HON. GEORGE OPDYKE.

FELLOW-CITIZENS—We have assembled for a high and holy purpose. We come to renew our vows at the altar of patriotism; and at what place so fitting as in the presence of a monument erected to the memory of Washington? [Cheers.] We come to reaffirm our earnest devotion to our country; to pledge our lives and all that we possess in defence of the Constitution and Union which our fathers bequeathed to us, and to declare our unalterable determination to defend them to the last, not merely against the assaults of traitors, but if need be against a world in arms. [Cheers.] Come what may, whether disaster or success, we are determined to "fight on, and fight ever," until a glorious and enduring triumph shall crown our efforts. [Cheers.]

We are here, too, to denounce treason and to disown political fellowship with all who sympathize with it. We have no toleration for those who, without provocation, have drenched our country in blood, in a fiendish attempt to overthrow a Government at once the mildest and most beneficent that human wisdom ever devised. History records no blacker crime against society. In a contest with such a foe there can be no middle or neutral ground. All who are not earnestly opposed to these enemies of their country and of the human race, must be regarded as participators in their guilt; all who apologize for their crime must share in the infamy that awaits them. Nor are there any grounds of compromise with such an enemy. Unconditional submission to the Constitution and laws they have contemned, is the only basis of reconciliation that honor or safety will permit us to offer them. [Cheers.]

We are here to stimulate and encourage the President, and all others charged with the duty of suppressing this infamous rebellion; to declare to the Administration our confidence in its honesty, ability and singleness of purpose; to bid it be of good cheer, for the people, regardless of all party affinities, have resolved that the Union must and shall be preserved, [loud cheers;] and that to this end, and the speedy suppression of the rebellion, they are prepared to stand as one man in support of the Administration in every advancing step it may take in earnestness of effort, and in the employment of every means justified by the usages of war. [Cheers.]

But, above all, we are here to rekindle the half-slumbering patriotism of our countrymen, and to urge them to respond with alacrity to the call of the Government for additional volunteers. A bitter and relentless foe is striking at its vitals, and appealing to the enemies of free government everywhere to aid in the unholy work. Their efforts will fail utterly and hopelessly. But to make that failure quick, sure, and overwhelming, let there be a general uprising and arming throughout the loyal States; and let this be followed by a prompt forward movement of the armies of the Union, so strong and irresistible that the armed traitors will be quickly driven to choose between flight and unconditional submission. [Enthusiastic cheering.]

D. D. FIELD, being called upon by the Chair, read the following

ADDRESS,

ADOPTED AND RECOMMENDED BY THE CONVENTION OF COMMITTEES.

The war in which the United States are engaged is not a war of conquest, but purely of defence. We are fighting for that which we received from our fathers: for the Union, which was freely entered into by all the parties to it: for the Constitution, which is older than this generation, which was made, in part, by the rebel States, and which every rebel leader has oftentimes sworn to support. We did not resist till our forbearance was imputed to pusillanimity: we did not strike till we had been struck; and when we took up arms, we sought only to retake that which had been taken from us by force, or surrendered by an imbecile or traitorous President and Cabinet.

The Rebellion had no cause or pretext which was even plausible. Misgovernment by the Federal power was not even pretended, nor any just apprehension of misgovernment, for, though a President had been chosen whose opinions were hostile to the extension of Slavery, the other departments of the Government were so constituted that no legislation hostile to the South could have been perfected. The Rebels revolted, therefore, against a Government which themselves or their fathers had, of their free choice, created for them, whose powers they had generally wielded, and whose offices they had for the greater part filled.

What this rebellion was for is declared by the Constitution which the rebels immediately adopted for themselves, and to which they invited the adhesion of the loyal States. That instrument may be regarded as their manifesto. It is for the most part a copy of the Constitution of the United States, with these two important additions—the perpetual servitude of the African race, and the inalienable right of each State to secede from the rest at will. Slavery and secession are the two corner-stones of the rebel constitution, the differences between that and our own, and, of course, the only causes and objects of the rebellion.

Whoever, therefore, either in this country, or in Europe, sympathizes with the rebels, or abets them, must justify the taking up of arms and filling the land with distress and slaughter, for the establishment of the perpetual right of slavery, and the perpetual right of secession. The bare statement of the proposition, so far as slavery is concerned, should seem to be a sufficient argument. In this age of the world, under the influence of our Christian civilization, it seems incredible that any set of men should dare to proclaim perpetual human servitude as a fundamental article of their social compact, or that any other man should be found on the face of the world to justify or even to tolerate them. In respect to the assumed right of secession, the argument is short and conclusive. Our Constitution established a Government and not a league; that was its purpose: the aim of its founders to make it a Government indissoluble and immortal, was as clearly expressed in the language of the instrument, and of contemporaneous writings, as it was possible to express it.

That man must be most ignorant of American history and law, who does not know that the idea of a league or partnership is wholly foreign to our constitutional system. The union between England and Scotland is as much a league or partnership, as the union between New-York and Virginia, and when Englishmen talk of the right of Virginia to self-government, let them ask themselves if they think Scotland has a right to secede from England at will.

So much for the legal right—now for the political necessity. The secession of Louisiana and Florida from Pennsylvania and Ohio can no more be admitted, considered as a question of policy alone, than could the secession of Wales from England, or Burgundy from France: nay, more, it would be possible for France to exist as a powerful empire, without a foot of the old domain of the Burgundian princes; and England might be powerful and respected, though the Welsh in their mountains still maintained their independence. But such is the shape of this continent, and the net-work of waters which flow through the Delta of the Mississippi into the Gulf of Mexico, that one part of the great valley cannot secede from the other. Providence has written its eternal decree upon the rivers and mountains of our continent, that the north-western and the south-western States shall be forever joined. But if it were possible to be otherwise—if several independent communities, without any national tie, could exist side by side in the great basin of our continent—they would be rivals, and from rivals would become enemies, warring with each other, seeking foreign alliances, obstructing each other's prosperity, and assailing each other's power. The great experiment of Republican Government would have failed ; an experiment depending for its success upon the possibility of uniting the independent action of separate States in respect to the greater number of the functions of government, with the action of a national government upon all matters of common concern.

If, as we believe, the fate of Republican Government in America is to determine whether a great country can be governed by any other than the monarchical form, with its concomitants of privileged classes, and standing armaments ; and, of course, whether this country of ours is to continue to be the asylum for the poor and the oppressed of all countries ; there can be no greater question presented to any people than that now presented to us ; none in which the millions of this continent, and of Europe, are more deeply concerned. If such a sacrifice were necessary, the thirty millions who now inhabit these States could do nothing so useful or sublime as to give themselves and all that they have, that they might leave this broad land under one free, indissoluble, republican government, opening wide its arms to the people of all lands, and promising happy homes to hundreds of millions for scores of ages.

We are persuaded that there has never been a struggle between authority and rebellion, whose issues involved more of good or ill to the human race. We are fighting not for ourselves alone, but for our fellow-men, and for the millions who are to come after us. These are scenes in the great war of opinion, which began before the century opened, and which will be ended only when it shall be decided whether government is for the few or the many.

We do not war with monarchical governments, or monarchical

principles. They may be the best for some countries. The Republican form of government is the one we prefer for ourselves, and for that, in its purity, and its strength, we are offering up our substance, and pouring out our blood like water. We are contending for that scheme of government for which Washington and the rest of the Fathers took up arms; for the integrity of our country, for our national existence, for the Christian civilization of our land, for our commerce, our arts, our schools; for all those earthly things which we have been taught most to cherish and respect.

Such being the magnitude of the stake in this contest, can it be wondered at, that we feel that all that we have, and all that we can do, should be given to our country in this its great hour of trial. If there be a man among us who does not feel thus, he should leave us. We cannot endure the thought of a traitor in the midst of us. For ourselves, we are willing to make every sacrifice necessary to secure the triumph of the Government. It can have all the resources of twenty millions of people. All we ask of it is, that it shall use them quickly, vigorously and wisely. Let us have no disunited counsels, no uncertain policy, no insufficient armaments, no paltering with rebellion. The crisis is most serious and imminent. The nation is not in a mood for trifling. It believes that the surest means of suppressing the rebellion are the best. It complains only of delays, vacillation, weakness. It wishes the strength of the nation to be collected, and when collected, used, so that not a vestige of revolt remain. We know that we have the men and the means; we only demand of the Government that it do what it is bound to do, use them with singleness of purpose, with well-considered plan, under the lead of the wisest counsel and the most skillful command.

This rebellion is a matter between ourselves and the rebels. No person other than an American has anything to do with it. If another intrudes into it, we must regard and treat him as an enemy. And if any foreign Government, forgetting its own duties, attempts to interfere in our affairs, the attempt must be repelled, as we are sure it will be repelled, with that firmness and spirit which become the American people and their representatives. If there be anything about which we are all agreed, it is the wisdom of our traditional policy, that we will not interfere in the affairs of other nations, nor allow their interference in ours. To the maintenance of this policy the nation is devoted, and the Government can count on the unanimous support of our people.

Forasmuch, then, as the actual rebellion and the possibility of foreign intervention make it necessary that the whole loyal people of this country should be banded together as one man, for the defence of all they hold most dear, we here pledge ourselves to each other, to Congress, and to the President, that, with all our resources, we will support the Government in the prosecution of this war, with the utmost possible vigor, till the rebellion is utterly overcome, and its leaders brought to merited punishment.

The Address was adopted by acclamation.

JOHN AUSTIN STEVENS, Jr., next read the following

RESOLUTIONS,

ADOPTED AND RECOMMENDED BY THE CONVENTION OF COMMITTEES.

WHEREAS, at a meeting of the citizens of New-York, convened on the 20th of April, 1861, it was resolved to support the Government in the prosecution of the war then opened by the rebels, with all the means in our power; and whereas, nothing has since occurred to change our opinions, or our determination then expressed, but everything to confirm them; and whereas, after a series of successes to the Federal arms, interrupted only by a few temporary reverses, the casualties of war have reduced the effective strength of the regiments in the field, so that recruits are needed to fill them up; and whereas, the occupation of the places repossessed by our army requires an additional force, and the President has called for three hundred thousand men, and for these reasons another meeting of citizens has been called, and is now assembled, it is thereupon

Resolved, That we reaffirm all the resolutions of the meeting of April, 1861, hereby declaring, that every event that has since occurred has served to strengthen the convictions, then held, of the wickedness of this rebellion, and the duty of all loyal citizens to suppress it with the strong hand, and at all hazards.

Resolved, That this war is waged on the part of the loyal for the overthrow only of the disloyal; that we seek not to enforce any claims or to establish any privileges beyond those given us by the Constitution of our fathers; and our only aim and purpose have been, and are now, to maintain the supremacy of that Constitution, over every foot of soil where it ever bore sway, with not a line interpolated, or a line erased.

Resolved, That we are for the union of the States, the integrity of the Country, and the maintenance of this Government, without any condition or qualification whatever; and we will stand by them and uphold them, under all circumstances, and at every necessary sacrifice of life or treasure.

Resolved, That while we recognize, and will sedulously maintain, the rights of each State under the Constitution, we abhor and repudiate the doctrine—fatal to national unity, and so prolific of treason in the army and navy, and among the people—that allegiance is due to the State, and not to the United States; holding it as a cardinal maxim, that to the United States, as a collective Government, is due the primary allegiance of all our people; and that any State or confederation of States, which attempts to divert it, by force or otherwise, is guilty of the greatest of crimes against humanity and our National Union.

Resolved, That we urge upon the Government the exercise of its utmost skill and vigor, in the prosecution of this war, unity of design, comprehensiveness of plan, a uniform policy and the stringent use of all the means within its reach, consistent with the usages of civilized warfare.

Resolved, That we acknowledge but two divisions of the people of the United States in this crisis; those who are loyal to its constitution and every inch of its soil, and are ready to make every sacrifice for the integrity of the Union, and the maintenance of civil liberty within it, and those who openly or covertly endeavor to sever our country, or to yield to the insolent demand of its enemies: that we fraternize with the former, and detest the latter; and that, forgetting all former party names and distinctions, we call upon all patriotic citizens to rally for one undivided country, one flag, one destiny.

Resolved, That the Government of the United States, and its people, with an occasional exception among the reckless inhabitants where this rebellion was fostered, have wisely and studiously avoided all interference with the concerns of other nations, asking, and usually enjoying, a like non-interference with their own, and that such is, and should continue to be, its policy; that the intimations of a contemplated departure from this sound rule of conduct on the part of some of the nations of Europe, by an intervention in our present struggle, is as unjust to them as it would be to us, and to the great principles for which we are contending; but we assure them, with a solemnity of conviction which admits of no distrust or fear, and from a knowledge of, and a firm reliance upon the spirit and fortitude of twenty millions of freemen, that any attempt thus to intervene, will meet a resistance unparalleled in its force, unconquerable in its persistence, and fatal to those whom it is intended to aid; and that it will tend only to strengthen and elevate the Republic.

Resolved, That the skill, bravery and endurance exhibited by our army and navy, have elicited our admiration and gratitude; that we behold in these qualities the assurances of sure and speedy success to our arms, and of rout and discomfiture to the rebels; that we urge the Government to aid and strengthen them by all the means in its power, and carefully to provide for sick, wounded and disabled soldiers and their families; to prosecute the war with increased vigor and energy, until the rebellion is utterly crushed, the integrity of the Union in all its borders restored, and every rebel reduced to submission, or driven from the land; and that to accomplish these ends, we pledge to our rulers, our faith, our fortunes, and our lives.

4

Resolved, That we approve of the administration of the President of the United States, and of the measures recommended and sanctioned by him for the prosecution of the war, the suppression of the rebellion, and the welfare of the country; that we sanction as wise and expedient the call for three hundred thousand more troops, and earnestly exhort our countrymen to rally to the standard of the Union, and bear it aloft until it shall float in peace and security, and be everywhere respected and honored.

Resolved, That a general armament is required by every consideration of policy and safety, and the Government should lose no time in filling up our armies and putting the whole sea-coast in a state of complete defence.

Resolved, That it be recommended to the Common Council of the city of New-York to offer a bounty of twenty-five dollars to every resident of the city, who shall within thirty days enlist into any regiment now in the field.

Which were unanimously adopted.

The next performance was the singing of "Our Country and her Flag," composed by FRANCIS LIEBER. For this purpose thousands of copies of the song were scattered among the crowd, being thrown from the main stand. The effect of this song, by a full chorus of manly voices, and with the accompaniment of the band, was very striking. The air is that of a glorious old anthem.

A SONG
ON OUR COUNTRY AND HER FLAG.

BY FRANCIS LIEBER.

Sung at the Meeting of Loyal Citizens, Union Square, New-York, July 15, 1862.

TUNE—*Gaudeamus igitur.*

We do not hate our enemy—
 May God deal gently with us all.
We love our land; we fight her foe;
 We hate his cause, and that must fall.

Our country is a goodly land;
 We'll keep her alway whole and hale;
We'll love her, live for her or die;
 To fall for her is not to fail.

Our Flag! The Red shall mean the blood
 We gladly pledge; and let the White
Mean purity and solemn truth,
 Unsullied justice, sacred right.

Its Blue, the sea we love to plow,
 That laves the heaven-united land,
Between the Old and Older World,
 From strand, o'er mount and stream, to strand.

The Blue reflects the crowding stars,
  Bright Union-emblem of the free ;
Come, all of ye, and let it wave—
  That floating piece of poetry.

Our fathers came and planted fields,
  And manly Law, and schools and truth ;
They planted Self-Rule, which we'll guard,
  By word and sword, in age, in youth.

Broad Freedom came along with them
  On History's ever-widening wings,
Our blessing this, our task and toil ;
  For " arduous are all noble things."

Let Emp'ror never rule this land,
  Nor fitful Crowd, nor senseless Pride.
Our Master is our self-made Law ;
  To *him* we bow, and none beside.

Then sing and shout for our free land,
  For glorious FREELAND'S victory :
Pray that in turmoil and in peace
  FREELAND our land may ever be ;

That faithful we be found, and strong,
  When History builds as corals build,
Or when she rears her granite walls—
  Her moles with crimson mortar filled.

The Chairman introduced Hon. CHARLES KING, who was welcomed with enthusiastic applause.

SPEECH OF THE HON. CHAS. KING, LL. D.

FELLOW-CITIZENS,—You see before you a man for many years withdrawn by the nature of his pursuits from all political affairs, but yet with a heart that beats as warmly toward the interest, and welfare, and honor of the country, as the youngest in this vast concourse. [Cheers.] I come before you, therefore, to speak in behalf of a cause common to every American heart. We are here to-day to co-operate in putting down the most wicked, wanton, causeless rebellion that ever offended the justice of God or stained the annals of man. [Applause.] We have been called upon by those in authority to send forth new regiments to the field, and recruits to the old regiments whom the fortune of war has decimated, and we come together now to pledge ourselves, that so far as each one of us is concerned, those men shall not be wanting, and those regiments shall be filled up. Can there be a more sacred cause than this? Can anything appeal more strongly to our interests, our feelings, our honor, our patriotism, than this? Can we submit to the shame and degradation of permitting our sons and our brothers who have gone forth at their country's call, to stand exposed and unaided, to be cut down and decimated by the enemy, while we are calmly carrying on our daily avocations at home? [Cries of "No, No."] Surely not; it cannot be! [Cries of "Never! Never!"] Let us resolve here, once for all, that we will support our brothers in the field—that we will put everything at hazard to conquer the Rebellion and re-establish the Union. [Cheers.] We have heretofore lacked in earnestness of purpose in the conduct of the war. We have dealt too mildly with those whom but a little while ago we regarded as our friends. They are no longer friends, but deadly enemies. They make war in earnest. They omit no means of strengthening their hands and weakening ours. They fight with no remembrance that we were once brothers. Why, then, should we remember it? They fight us like incarnate fiends; let us, at least, meet them as our deadliest foes. [Applause.] Let us now go forth and make the war as fierce and bloody as it is possible for a civilized nation to make it. No moderation is shown to us; let us show none to them. We are far more powerful in numbers, and better prepared than our enemies. We have heretofore acted too much on the defensive; let us now act on the offensive. [Cheers.] Let us henceforth strike rapid and constant blows— blows that shall tell. Let us no longer hear that the Army of the Potomac is "safe." Safe! Great God! The army should be triumphant. [Loud applause.] We have no criticism to make. I only speak common-sense when I say that war is a fierce game; that they only prevail who wage it in earnest. War cannot be waged in silken gloves. When we send forth our armies, it must be understood that they go to battle.

Gentlemen, I speak to you as a citizen of New-York, older than any one that I look upon here, quite as much interested in everything that concerns the city and the country as any of you. Indeed, I have done almost everything that a man of my age can do to give success to the war. I have sent sons and grandsons to it, and I am ready, if necessary, to go myself. [Loud cheers.] And I promise you that neither of those sons will ever dishonor the name he bears or the education he received. [Cheers.] They are false friends and pernicious counselors who, in so great a cause as this, would interpose side issues, and would seek to advance mean and miserable personal or party aims and ambitions, by sowing the seeds of discord and jealousy among our public men, whether in civil or military life. Let all such discussion—all intermediate questions or discussion, which of necessity must be subordinate to the great and vital question of our National existence, which is now in the debate of arms—be postponed till the battle is won. *Then* there will be a great nation—calm in conscious strength, to judge and to determine all political questions. *Now*, let there be only a nation of soldiers, resolved upon trampling treason in the dust, and eager and earnest for aggressive war. Aggressive, I repeat, in every form that the laws of war permit. Now our armies in the field are made the special guardians for the benefit of rebel women and children—of the property which the husbands and fathers have abandoned in order to join the rebel army—and upon many a bloody field our wounded and dying have been obliged to put up with such wayside fare and nourishment as the chance of battle left for them, while hard by, rebel houses, and rebel gardens, and rebel granaries, abounding in comforts which might have saved life, and certainly would have mitigated suffering, are sacredly guarded by our troops for the benefit of the rebel families. This may be magnanimous, but it is not war. I would have all this changed. [Cheers.]

I am for the war in its fiercest form—always and in all things, however, having regard to our own character and superior civilization. [Applause.] Our antagonists claim that they are the *master race*, and, as such, entitled to rule the land and give law to the baser sort, whom, as by one general term of reproach, they stigmatize as Yankee. This claim of superiority, indeed, was announced in a recent article of one of the leading newspapers in Richmond, as among the determining causes of this rebellion. We of the North, it was said, confident in our numbers and wealth, seemed to forget that we were an inferior race, and to be disposed to throw off the yoke of the chivalry, and set up for ourselves; and thence the necessity, it was argued, that the master race should assert its supremacy, and bring us back to wonted submissiveness. The Yankee must be made to take off his hat when in the presence of a Southern gentleman! Perhaps so! But before that lesson is learned, a good many Southern heads will fall. Why, in every element that constitutes true manhood—in physical power, in educated mind, in religious instruction, in habits of self-command, in the dignity of bread-winning industry, in the knowledge of his own rights, and in respect for the rights of others—in all that constitutes a man and a citizen—the Northern race is far, very far, superior to the Southern race. [Cheers.] With this moral and physical superiority, how can it be otherwise than that, admitting equal courage on both sides, (and that is a generous concession to the South,) with our great preponderance of numbers, we must, when once fairly aroused, effectually subdue them? [Cheers.]

We are to listen to no talk of compromise, of negotiation, and, least of all, of foreign mediation. Compromise of what? Our right to exist as a nation? for that is the whole question. Negotiation with whom? Rebels in arms, traitors that have struck at the bosom of our common mother! And who among us would listen for an instant to mediation on the part of either France or England? [Loud cheers, and cries of "No one!"] Under what pretence of right shall either of those nations, or both together, venture to interfere in our domestic quarrel? It is an offensive assumption of European superiority which we will not brook. We are a people of ourselves, and by ourselves—competent to manage our own affairs, without the aid or counsel of others—owing allegiance to God—but none to any earthly powers—and thoroughly resolved to submit to no dictation or intervention from any such powers.

No, friends, this is no time for parley, for negotiation, for half-way measures of any sort. The people are far ahead of the Government. They are in earnest, and will not be paltered with; they mean to put down the rebellion, and to punish the traitors with the most condign punishment. They have a policy, whoever else may lack one. They mean war, in earnest, and they mean that war deals with men only as friends and as enemies. [Applause.] It has no cognizance of political questions, of social institutions; it deals plainly and directly with men, and the only question it asks of them, without regarding race or color, is, " Are you for us or against us?" If for us, come and help; if against us, we shall know how to deal with you. This is war, according to common-sense and universal usage. A general in the field is bound to succeed, and in order to that to use all lawful means conducive to success. He may take the life—none deny that—of the enemy. Shall he, then, hesitate about taking his property whenever and wherever it can be useful to his own force? [Cheers.]

He may seize his crops, his cattle, and why not his slaves? What right has a general in the field to expose our sons and our brothers to the horrors of unequal war, when thousands stand ready to help him if he will only say the word? A general in the field knows nothing of slavery—that is a political and social question, with which it is none of his business to deal. He has to do only with the means of successfully prosecuting war, and wherever these means are to be found he must use them. This is so plain, that but for the prejudice of color none would hesitate about it; and yet it is not conceivable that the existence, possibly, of this great Continental Republic, the lives of our sons and brothers, should depend upon a question of complexion. If the issue be between the preservation of the Union and the preservation of slavery, who shall hesitate? It may, indeed, be—who shall say that it is not?—within the inscrutable purposes of Providence that, whereas all this great disaster and crime arises from slavery and the disappointed, mad ambition of slaveholding leaders, the result of this dire conflict shall be the total extinction of the great evil which has thus culminated in the greater crime of rebellion?

But of that I am not here to speak. All I urge is, that in the war to the death we use all the means which, according to all the usage of civilized war, we are entitled to use; and that while our adversaries stop at no expedients to strengthen their hands, we shall not weaken ours by half-way, halting, mean and miserable hesitations.

See to it, you my friends; let us all, individually and collectively, see to it that henceforth the lightning's flash shall tell of assault, of battle, of victory—of the enemy overthrown and subdued—of our old and honored flag restored in all its amplitude to every contested point throughout the land—of treason vanquished, and of the Union reaffirmed and consolidated. Men of New-York, this you can greatly help to do. Fail not, then, as you value your peace on earth, your hopes of Heaven. [Prolonged applause.]

After music by the band, WM. ROSS WALLACE spoke, with thrilling and dramatic effect, an ode prepared by him for the occasion. The following is the

ODE
BY WILLIAM ROSS WALLACE.

Keep step with the music of Union,
  The music our ancestors sung,
When States, like a jubilant chorus,
  To beautiful sisterhood sprung!
O! thus shall their great Constitution,
  That guards all the homes of the land,
A mountain of freedom and justice,
  For millions eternally stand.

  North and South, East and West, all unfurling
    ONE Banner alone o'er the sod,
  ONE voice from America swelling
    In worship of Liberty's God!

Keep step with the music of Union,
What grandeur its flag has unrolled—
For the loyal, a star-lighted Heaven,
For traitors, a storm in each fold!
The glorious shade of Mount Vernon
Still points to each patriot's grave,
Still cries—" O'er the long mighty ages
That Eagle of Lexington wave."
North and South, East and West, &c.

Keep step with the music of Union,
The forests have sunk at the sound.
The pioneer's brows been with triumph
And Labor's broad opulence crowned ;
Oh! yet *must* all giant rude forces
Of Nature be chained to our cars—
All mountains, lakes, rivers and oceans
Crouch under the Stripes and the Stars.
North and South, East and West, &c.

Keep step with the music of Union,
Thus still shall we nourish the light
Our fathers lit for the chained nations
That darkle in Tyranny's night!
The blood of the whole world is with us.
O'er ocean by Tyranny hurled,
And they who would dare to insult us
Shall sink with the wrath of the world.
North and South, East and West, &c.

Keep step with the music of Union,
All traitors shall fall at our march.
But patriots bask in the blessing
Flashed down from yon heavenly arch!
Then hurrah for the Past with its glory!
For the strong, earnest Present, hurrah!
And a cheer for the starry browed Future
With Freedom, and Virtue, and Law.
*North and South, East and West all unfurling
One Banner alone o'er the sod,
One voice from America swelling
In worship of Liberty's God!*

SPEECH OF GEN. HIRAM WALBRIDGE.

Gen. WALBRIDGE was then introduced, by his Honor the Mayor; who observed, that he would present to them their distinguished fellow-citizen, who as early as April, 1861, was in favor of calling, at once, six hundred thousand men to suppress the rebellion. Gen. WALBRIDGE said :—

MR. MAYOR, FRIENDS AND FELLOW-CITIZENS :

Fourteen months ago, from this very platform, the city of New-York, in the presence of a quarter of a million of loyal citizens, declared that she would not sit tamely by and behold a wicked, reckless, malignant minority consummate the overthrow and ruin of the only representative constitutional Government on earth. When she fixed this determination, and announced her will, eleven rebellious States had attempted to sever their connection with the Federal Government; had torn from the forts, arsenals, magazines and harbors within their limits the banner of the constitutional Union. This reckless, rampant treason, though long threatened, took the civilized world by surprise; and, as the conspirators by thousands poured their murderous hail of shot and shell upon that thirsty, half-famished garrison at Fort Sumter, with its seventy exhausted but loyal men, they little realized that throughout the whole Christian world they were calling silently into exercise forces wholly beyond human control; for that man must be an atheist, or have no soul, who does not realize, that since that first event God himself has been manifest in the moral and political phenomena which this great, loyal nation now presents, and statesmen, and philosophers, and generals, will begin to reason right and act right, when they realize this great truth. The establishment of free institutions on this continent toward ameliorating the condition of the human race, was second to the inauguration of the Christian religion, and their dismemberment and overthrow is reserved only to Jehovah himself.

Fellow-citizens, when last we met here, on the occasion to which I have referred, bold, rank, audacious treason pervaded almost every department of the Federal service. Army, navy, embassadors to foreign courts, collectors of customs, postmasters, the very defences at Washington, limited as they were, could not then be relied upon. The nation trembled for the safety of the national capital; the personal safety of the President was endangered even in the Executive mansion. Consternation and despair briefly ruled the hour. How stands the matter now? The capital is secured; the rebels are trembling for Charleston, Savannah, and their entire coast, while we have New Orleans and Nashville. Delaware, Maryland, Kentucky, and Missouri, then on the verge of rebellion, are secured; Virginia, then completely in the grasp of the rebels, has become loyal in the greater portion of her territorial extent. Over eight hundred thousand troops have been called into the field, armed, equipped, and provided, equal to any army ever before called into service; a navy, like Pallas, from the brain of Jove, seems to have sprung at once into complete existence; three thousand miles of coast have been blockaded, and a landing has been effected upon the soil of that pestiferous State, which first instigated and finally produced this wicked rebellion. I would that we could here have first made our terrible visitation of the power and resources of the Federal Government in quelling the treason, firmly believing, had that been done, the border States would never have hesitated in their allegiance. Twenty millions of people are on the one side, backed by the consciousness they are contending for the integrity and maintenance of the Government from which they have achieved greatness and commanded respect throughout the world. Eight millions of rebels oppose them. The grounds of the contest are clearly defined—treason, revolt and anarchy are on the one side; liberty, security and prosperity on the other. Great as is the disparity in wealth and numbers, the traitors thus far have maintained the unequal contest. But the end is not yet. An additional

300,000 troops have been called into requisition by our exigencies. This patriotic action of the Government must be sustained, traitors at home must be punished, spies and informers must be annihilated, the Union must be preserved, and condign punishment afterward inflicted upon all who have taken this period in our history to fatten upon the misfortunes of the Republic. A broad and beneficent statesmanship must be adopted, and the policy of the Government must be borne upon our victorious standards as they advance into the rebel territory. That policy should be broad, national and statesmanlike; but it should be so rapid, so powerful, so wise, and so energetic, that the national life will survive, and the authority of the Constitution in the rebellious States be recognized, if to accomplish it every existing institution, order, monopoly, or privilege, should be swept before our advancing hosts. Rights should be recognized, privileges discarded, and the authority of the United States floating again over its former territorial limits, its flag everywhere emblazoned in characters of living light—"The Union, it must and shall be preserved." It is to be seriously deplored that at this juncture our fears are appealed to lest the proportions of this contest shall be largely augmented by some efforts at intervention from foreign powers, which may result in collision in our present domestic dissensions. From the first dawning of our domestic dissensions the governing class in England have desired, not their repression, but their increase, and have actively sympathized with these internal traitors to dismember our Government. They thus hope to render the people of North America as impotent to oppose their political and commercial domination as similar domestic contentions have already reduced the people of the South American Republics. Hence at the very commencement of the rebellion the English ministry made haste to recognize the rebels as belligerents, and to place them on the same level as the Government against which they had rebelled. Intervene to make peace! Intervention will deluge the earth with blood. This country cannot be dismembered but by subjugation, amid seas of blood and oceans of flame. Never. England and France combined, with what is left of the rebels, cannot subjugate and dismember the United States. In such an atrocious attempt every lover of liberty and fair dealing in Europe will be our friend; every hater of British tyranny will be our friend; every hater of Napoleon will be our friend; the Pope would rejoice to see the end of a dynasty which seeks his degradation; Venice would find herself a part of Italy, and Austria would find a compensation in exemption from future dangers on the Rhine, and in a division with Russia of the "sick man's estate." Intervene for humanity! Transparent falsehood! The United States will neither be subjugated or dismembered while the loyal American people remain true to their Revolutionary origin. But as becomes wise and practical men, we should closely examine the means of assault and the means of defence if this burden should be forced upon us; and here again we shall witness abundant opportunity for confidence and hope. It is fair to assume, should intervention ever come, the two Western powers of France and England will act in unison, as they did in the Crimean war, and as they have recently co-operated with Spain by intervening with the internal affairs of Mexico. These two powers combined possess a large army. If undisturbed, in from eight to nine months, by gigantic efforts and at vast cost, they might ferry across the Atlantic from 240,-000 to 275,000 soldiers, with all their armaments and supplies. This would, however, be doing far more than they were able to do in the Crimean war, though largely aided by American steam transport ships. At no time in the year can they in one voyage readily transport 100,000 soldiers, and the immense amount of necessary arms and supplies. Even if able to shelter their soldiers till the last detachment arrives, and all move together, some nine or ten months after hostilities should arise they would stand in the presence of disciplined troops twice as numerous as themselves—in the presence of troops who have fought far more battles against resolute troops than themselves—a few thousand French troops alone excepted.

The American troops—regiment for regiment—six months from to-day, will be as well drilled, in better condition and practice, will have seen more active service and as many battles, and will be better armed, than the regiments to which they will stand opposed, and will be more than twice as numerous. Their next means of assault consists in vessels of war—numerous and powerful—and, in addition, the English have constructed canals from the St. Lawrence into the great chain of American lakes, to enable them to convey gun-boats into these waters. We have no such connection with the ocean. They can transport their gun-boats among our commercial vessels, and in front of our interior cities, along a lake coast of more than two thousand miles, unopposed. We have nothing at this time—absolutely nothing—with which to oppose them on these great inland seas. But, per contra, we have to-day more armored vessels—genuine iron-clad—than both France and England. That much good has come out of this evil rebellion. In a few weeks— not months—we shall be able to teach the English, if they demand it of us, a new version of the naval lessons of 1812. Six or eight of our armored vessels can readily destroy the entire unarmored fleet of England. We shall soon have afloat iron-clad vessels, armed with carefully tested ordnance, carrying elongated projectiles with "punch points," of four hundred and eighty pounds, fully competent—first, to resist the concentrated fire of the Warrior, aided by the La Gloire, Napoleon's largest iron-clad ship; and second, by the use of shot alone to sink both of them, should they come within its range. We now have on hand the tested ordnance competent to speedily destroy any vessel yet armored by any nation. Our iron-clads are the most numerous at this time, and cannot be exceeded prior to January or February next. The English troops are dispersed all over the world to guard isolated colonies. Her available troops cannot be massed to an amount of eighty thousand; and one hundred and fifty thousand, if she had them, would not be troublesome to a powerful nation, possessing from 800,000 to 1,000,000 of troops already called to the field; and the French army, once shut on shipboard, even if convoyed by the whole English and French fleet, could not in an ordinarily fair fight escape destruction. A single conflict between an English or a French iron-clad and one of our far more heavily armed iron-clads will settle that question. The result will be so decisive as to admit of no mistake, if there is any virtue in ordnance throwing projectiles four times heavier than any approved gun with which any English or French vessel is now armed. Let us examine our means of defence. Of course, before going into battle, a soldier puts on his armor; when a man leaves home he locks the doors of his house. So a nation going to war with a naval enemy, will, at an early day, carefully lock the mouths of all those valuable harbors, inlets, sounds, and rivers, which have narrow entrances, and thus lessen the home duties of the fleet, as well as furnish a place of refuge when disabled by storms, or pressed by superior force. The mode of obstructing entrances to harbors, so as to effectually secure them, and yet allow of a passage of a friendly ship with but little hindrance, is pointed out with great clearness by the Board of Engineers in a report made to the Secretary of War in 1840. The obstruction can be created in the entrance to a harbor like that of New-York in probably two or three days. The whole British navy could not force a passage through the entrance, without first removing the obstruction; and the obstruction could be removed by an enemy only after the silencing of the forts under the command of whose guns it is placed. Having taken steps to carefully secure the most important entrance by temporary obstructions and by heavily armed forts, let us promptly provide an interior water communication between our chief cities, parallel with our Atlantic coast, and having numerous communications with it at protected points. This has been frequently recommended by the Board of Engineers as a work of vast military importance. In April last, the Military Committee of Congress, in an able report, demonstrated how this object could be speedily and cheaply accomplished, viz.: By enlarging the locks of three short canals, of an aggregate length of only 78½ miles. A vessel entering the sound of North Carolina, from the Atlantic Ocean, can proceed by way of the Dismal Swamp Canal (22 miles long) to Norfolk; then passing up the Chesapeake Bay, communicating with both Washington and Baltimore, if desirable, it can sail into the Delaware River through a canal only 13½ miles long; after communicating with the great city of Philadelphia, it could sail directly into New-York harbor, by passing through the Delaware and Raritan Canal, a distance of 43 miles, and thence proceed up the East River, 140 miles, to New London, before going to sea. Here is an inland communication between almost all of our leading ports and cities along the maritime front of the populous and powerful States of Connecticut, New-York, New Jersey, Pennsylvania, Delaware, Maryland, Virginia, and North Carolina—a distance of nearly 1,000 miles, and having many facile and easily protected outlets to the sea. Suitable timber locks, capable of passing large war vessels, can be made ready for use, in a case of pressing emergency, in from twenty to twenty-five days. The Government has ample legal authority to make this great improvement, if a military necessity. As it is, let it be done, and in such a manner that we can easily concentrate large ships at any desirable harbor to resist any invasion, when the telegraph shall announce the disasters or separations wrought on the enemy's fleet by storms or by our returning squadrons. The engineers strongly recommend this double coast line as a remarkable military advantage possessed by neither England nor France. Our own sense tells us that if a ship or ships of war or commerce should be blockaded in a harbor, and thus prevented from going to sea, the evil would be lessened if the harbor was connected, by a safe and unexposed interior channel, with all the harbors on the coast for a thousand miles—so also a blockade of one harbor could be broken up, by quietly concentrating in it a superior force drawn from the other harbors connected with it by the interior channel.

Let us also earnestly request the Government to aid in opening the communication for our iron gun-boats from the Mississippi to the Hudson, the Delaware and St. Lawrence. Then in the event of war, our iron-clad ships from the West, through the loyal States, could sail directly into the lakes, proceed to the head of the St. Lawrence, and protect the crossing of an army sufficiently powerful to command that river as low down as Montreal, and thus prevent a single British soldier from penetrating the interior. This accomplished, what amount of opposition could the unaided and defenseless Canadians make to our Western troops? The navigable waters of Canada secured, this inland fleet could forthwith repair to the aid of our defences at the mouth of the Hudson. A period of from ten to twenty days would place them at either point. In thirty days, in despite of the utmost efforts of England, the United States could control the upper St. Lawrence and the whole chain of lakes, for they have no iron-clads competent to navigate those waters, and to meet our superb Western iron-clad fleet, with its 11, 13 and 15 inch guns. Since the inauguration upon the waters of the Chesapeake, of a new era in the art of naval warfare, we have placed our country at the head of naval powers in effective strength, and the mechanical force of the country, for the time being, should be called into requisition in enlarging and strengthening the navy; and the comprehensive policy should be adopted of allowing the merchant marine to aid in its own defence by its incorporation into a militia navy, under proper laws and restrictions. We ought now to commence, and complete within six months, a heavy fleet of iron-clads of superior speed, and at least twice the capacity of the Monitor: and of the three millions of enrolled militia in the loyal States, with one million in the field, we may confidently anticipate bringing this infamous Rebellion to a triumphant close. With such an army and navy, with the forts armed with the modern improved ordnance of large calibre; with the valuable inlets to harbors, roadsteads and sounds, skillfully obstructed; with an interior water communication between the several ports and harbors on the Atlantic, so as to make it safe and convenient to speedily pass a fleet from one to another entirely beyond the observation of any enemy lying off a fort; with a navigable communication between New-York bay and the lakes, and between the lakes and St. Louis and New Orleans, that would allow of a movement of the whole fleet from New Orleans to New-York, or from New-York to New Orleans, by an inland route free from danger and observation, surely we can maintain our national unity and our national honor. But I must draw these remarks to a close. New-York again to-day, as at the beginning of the struggle, demonstrates that she is still loyal to the Government and the Constitution. She feels the deepest sympathy for the martyred dead, who have fallen in defence of constitutional, well-regulated liberty. As the tidings of this great gathering are borne throughout the loyal camps, it will animate the heart and nerve the arm of our brave and intrepid soldiers. In behalf of that immense army of privates, who have left home and kindred and friends, to meet the traitors striking at the heart of the nation, and who never mean to abandon this contest until the old flag again floats over every inch of our original territorial limit, I ask you to send them the cheering words of your hearty commendation.

Gen. WALBRIDGE was cheered throughout most enthusiastically, and as he was concluding, said he had prepared some resolutions, which he would read and if they met the approval of this vast, intelligent and patriotic assemblage, he would request the MAYOR to ask for their adoption. As Gen. WALBRIDGE read each one, cheer after cheer welcomed them, and when the last was concluded, the whole vast assemblage gave one unbroken and hearty Yea. The MAYOR then formally offered them again, when they were carried, amidst the most tumultuous and enthusiastic applause.

Resolved, That the territorial limits of the United States, as they existed before this infamous rebellion began, and the Constitution which guarantees their existence, should forever remain one, entire, united and indivisible.

Resolved, That the division of the former, and the overthrow of the latter, would constitute a damning crime to all eternity.

Resolved, That as the blood of our slaughtered citizen soldiers, fallen in defence of constitutional liberty, cries to Heaven for redress, we declare that, to suppress this Rebellion and save the national life. the Government should call into exercise every agency employed by the Rebels themselves to make the war effective, conclusive and of short duration.

Resolved, That we tender to our unfortunate countrymen, now languishing by captivity in Southern prisons, our earnest and cordial sympathy, and we beseechingly implore the Government to effect their honorable exchange and release at the earliest possible moment.

Resolved, That since integrity by public servants in the discharge of official duty is the only guaranty for good government, we call upon Congress to give the authority, and the Government to execute it, by hanging upon a gibbet higher than ever Haman hung, every official in any department of the public service, who attempts at this juncture of our public affairs to fatten upon the misfortunes of the Republic, either by defrauding the public Treasury, employing his public position to advance private pecuniary objects, or who shall be found guilty of imposing upon our brave soldiers any base article either in the food or raiment provided for them by the Government.

Resolved, That Congress should provide for opening the great line of interior water communication along our Atlantic coast, capable of passing our naval fleet and our commercial marine from the waters of the Roanoke and Chesapeake Bay to the eastern terminus of Long Island, and should at once open the means of internal communication, by which our gun-boats can pass from the Mississippi through the loyal States, by the various canals and lakes, until they reach the Atlantic sea-board, by the most cheap and expeditious routes that scientific and practical knowledge may develop.

Resolved, That our commercial marine, now largely in advance of any other nation, should be so organized as to aid in the means of its own defence, and that it is the duty of Congress to provide for this by incorporating a portion of the same into a "Militia of the Seas," and thus inaugurate a new element of National strength and defence, commensurate with our growing importance as a great leading maritime power.

Resolved, That steadily pursuing the wise policy of our fathers, we never mean to interfere in the internal conflicts of foreign States, but here, beneath this outstretched sky, in the presence of Almighty God, and of one another, we pledge our lives, our fortunes, and our sacred honor, never to abandon this struggle while there remains a traitor in the land; and that any armed intervention by any foreign power in our present domestic affliction, shall prove the signal for the spirit of Liberty to commence its triumphant march through Europe.

On the part of the Chairman, Mr. JOHN AUSTIN STEVENS, Jr., announced the following resolution, which was unanimously adopted:

Resolved, That this meeting cordially unites in recommending to the Governor and Legislature of this State, to take the earliest means of pledging the State to the payment of an additional bounty to volunteers.

The Star-Spangled Banner was then sung by the chorus and band, thousands of voices joining in the stirring refrain.

Mr. DUNN was next introduced, and after a few preliminary and patriotic remarks, read a poem, from which the following is an extract:

> Only once in every lifetime comes the hour for man to prove
> The depth, the truth, the earnestness of patriotic love;
> Only once in every lifetime comes the people thrilling jar
> That purifies the nation in the crucible of war;
> Which vindicates the honor of the Truth and proves the might
> Of the never-thwarted purpose which is founded in the right,
> And God will safely guard the man and make him doubly strong,
> Who battles in the cause of Right against the cause of Wrong.
> To the camp-enshrined Potomac, to its blood-stained, throbbing strand,
> Points the plain, unerring finger of God's invocating hand,
> And I hear the thrilling voices of the martyrs, one by one,
> Saying, "FREEMEN! On to glory, while there's labor to be done!"
> And can I stand here idle while I hear my country's call?
> While I see the gloom of treason 'round the Union's temple fall?
> No! I'll grasp the sword of duty, and move onward in the van,
> To the deeds which bless THE AGES and uphold the RIGHTS OF MAN!

SPEECH OF EX-SENATOR SPINOLA.

Ex-Senator SPINOLA, having been introduced to the meeting, on coming forward was warmly received. He said:—

I did not come here this day to make a speech to you. No, I come for a nobler purpose and a more important object. I come to ask you to join with me. (Hear, and applause.) The hour has arrived when it becomes the duty of every American citizen to buckle on his armor and go forward to the fight. (Loud cheers.) I have now, since our last glorious meeting in this place, witnessed the progress of this wretched rebellion, and my only regret is that a sufficient force was not then at once raised to drive the fomenters of it out of the country, and forever to keep it down. You are once more again gathered together in a great mass meeting to frustrate its future progress, and I call upon you to do your duty to your country in this the hour of her peril. (Applause, and cries of "We shall do so.") There were those who, at the last great mass meeting of New-York, were pretended friends to the Union, but who, I regret to state, as matters have since turned out, were the vilest snakes of treason. (Hear, and loud cheers.) Let our Northern States fall into Southern hands—let them sway the destinies of this mighty and world-famed republic—and if ever the day should arise when such a state of things should happen, not even man, woman or child would receive the slightest mercy at the hands of those Southern rebels. (Cries of "That's true—go on, Spinola.") Give them, I say, the upper hand, and the people of the North will soon feel the effects of Southern steel. But let them come on—I ask them to do so ; and if we have the real principles of freedom at heart, we shall soon teach them what virtue is in Northern arms. (Applause.) There is another great consideration in which we are all deeply interested. Let the South be successful and the North will not only have to pay the expenses of the rebellion, but to live in thralldom under their bloody sceptre. (Hear, hear.) As I said at the commencement of these remarks, I told you that I wished you to join with me in endeavoring to crush this awful rebellion. (Cries of "And so we will.") I have already determined, as you all know, to bear my humble part in this war, and in crushing the rebellion. I shall do so ; and should I meet with or discover any poor Southern wretch peculating the property of our gallant Northern troops, I will not go to the trouble of gibbeting him, but he shall suffer at the point of the bayonet. (Applause.) In connecting myself with the great Union army, I promise that the men whom I may be appointed to command shall receive my best attention. In the hour of danger and also of sickness I hope to stand by them, and to see that their wants are well cared for. Their wounds shall be skillfully attended to. (Loud cheers.) I look upon these duties as incumbent upon every commander to considerately carry out. Let us recollect those great men who gave us this government, and if we do we cannot but respect their memories. We are, the most of us, well acquainted with what they passed through. This should stimulate us in fighting hard in defence of the great Constitution which they formed on so permanent a basis. We are a well equipped body of men ; our military reputation cannot be excelled, and we are the best men in arms in the world. (Loud cheering.) I am now raising a brigade to join the great army of the North, and before long I hope that I shall be ready to head that brigade to the glorious battle-field. (Hear, hear.) After a few other remarks the ex-Senator concluded his address by calling on those present, who felt a desire to join his brigade, at once to do so. He said : I promise them every indulgence and encouragement, and so long as they fight under one flag—the glorious flag of the Union—they shall be secured in these. (Great applause.)

MR. BANVARD'S ADDRESS.

Mr. BANVARD was next introduced to the meeting, and said :—

PATRIOTIC FELLOW-CITIZENS,—I want to let you know that I have some knowledge of secession, and shall crave your indulgence for only a short time. Humphrey Marshall, of Kentucky, happened to move up with ten thousand men, but he was not long until he moved down again. (Loud cheers and laughter.) I know him personally, and I have very little to say in his favor, only that he soon discovered his mistake and did not make a second attempt. (Loud cheers.) I know the spirit of secession well, and have seen its workings. I have no hesitation whatever in declaring that its object is to uproot the principles of free government in this country, which have been so securely established by the first founders of that glorious, happy, and free Constitution. (Loud cheers.) Would time permit I could enter more into detail, but shall content myself with these few remarks.

The proceedings were here closed, and the meeting adjourned.

OFFICERS.

STAND No. 2.

Under charge of Committee of Arrangements.

PROSPER M. WETMORE. SAMUEL SLOAN.

President.

PELATIAH PERIT, *President of the Chamber of Commerce.*

Vice-Presidents.

ROYAL PHELPS,
A. A. LOW,
JOHN A. STEVENS,
JOHN C. GREEN,
ROBERT B. MINTURN,
JOHN D. WOLFE,
JAMES W. OTIS,
HENRY J. RAYMOND,
T. H. FAILE,
JAMES G. KING,
JOSEPH W. ALSOP,
MOSES TAYLOR,
BENJAMIN R. WINTHROP,
JAMES GALLATIN,
WILLIAM A. BOOTH,
SHEPHERD KNAPP,
R. A. WITTHAUS,
E. E. MORGAN,
ROBERT L. KENNEDY,
RICHARD W. WESTON,
MANTON MARBLE,
J. SMITH HOMANS,
W. W. DE FOREST,
WILSON G. HUNT.
SAMUEL D. BABCOCK,
HENRY F. VAIL,
H. W. T. MALI,
JACOB HERRICK,
CHARLES KING,
JOHN S. GILES,
M. MARBLE,
JOSIAH SUTHERLAND,
EDWIN J. BROWN,
F. SCHROEDLER,
W. H. LEONARD,
FREDERICK A. COE,

JOHN JACOB ASTOR, Jr.,
HENRY A. HURLBUT,
FRANCIS W. SKIDDY,
WILLARD PARKER,
SAMUEL T. SKIDMORE,
WILLIAM C. GILMAN,
E. V. HAUGHWOUT,
WILLIAM WATSON,
D. T. INGRAHAM,
JOHN RAYMOND,
PHILIP DATER, Jr.,
SAMUEL P. WILLIAMS,
GEORGE BLISS, Jr.,
U. A. MURDOCK,
JNO. L. HASBROUCK,
GEO. W. BRAINERD,
AUSTIN L. SANDS,
LEMUEL W. HOPKINS,
SAMUEL B. WHITE,
MOSES M. LAIRD,
GEORGE O. TOTTEN,
NATHAN KINGSLEY,
CHESTER A. ARTHUR,
JOHN HEWETT,
WILLIAM B. TAYLOR,
JAMES RENWICK, Jr.,
JAMES A. ROOSEVELT,
BENJ. ARNOLD,
JACOB NEVINS,
WILLIAM J. CORWIN,
LUCIUS TUCKERMAN,
JOSEPH P. VARNUM, Jr.,
WILLIAM B. HOFFMAN,
DAVID MILLER,
D. C. HAYES,
EUGENE KETELTAS.

ALFRED COLVILL,
ABRAHAM M. COZZENS,
THEODORE L. MASON,
R. D HITCHCOCK,
JOHN H. SWIFT,
GEO. CLARK,
A. B. HAYS,
JAMES OLIVER,
ALBERT SPEYERS,
ANDREW MATHEWS,
ROBERT L. McINTYRE,
JOHN WARREN,
PAUL S. FORBES,
TIMOTHY G. CHURCHILL,
E. CAYLUS,
ROBERT S. HONE.
RICHARD D. LATHROP,
WILLIAM HALL,

DANIEL B. FEARING,
CHARLES A. BRISTED,
JUSTUS DILL,
JAMES B. TAYLOR,
GEORGE OSGOOD,
CHARLES E. BEEBE,
EDWARD MINTURN,
CHAS. L. TIFFANY,
GEORGE S. PARKER,
GEORGE ANTHON,
JAMES GERARD,
WILLIAM KELLOCK,
OSCAR COLES,
SAMUEL D. BRADFORD,
F. S. LATHROP,
JOSEPH LEE,
JAMES UDALL,
HAMILTON BRUCE.

Secretaries.

EDWARD C. BOGERT,
J. SMITH HOMANS, Jr.,
HENRY I. BARBEY,
GEORGE D. LYMAN,
IRVING GRINNELL,
WILLIAM E. DODGE, Jr.,
WILLIAM H. GRENELLE,
WALKER BURNS,
J. HOWARD WILLIAMS,
ANDREW WARNER,
FRANK SHEPHERD,
LOUIS BELLONI, Jr.,
JOHN H. DRAPER,

TEMPLE PRIME,
BLEECKER OOTHOUT.
GEO. WILSON,
EDWARD WILLETS,
FRANK OTIS,
WASHINGTON COSTER,
DAVID BISHOP,
ANDREW H. SANDS,
JOHN W. MINTURN,
HENRY KETELTAS,
JOSEPH P. NORRIS, Jr.,
EDWARD S. RENWICK.

PROGRAMME OF PROCEEDINGS.

STAND No.

SALUTES OF ARTILLERY by ANTHON LIGHT BATTERY and by the WORKMEN employed by HENRY BREWSTER & CO.

1. MUSIC—Grand March.

2. PROSPER M. WETMORE will call the meeting to order, read the CALL FOR THE MEETING, and conduct to the Chair PELATIAH PERIT, President of the Chamber of Commerce.

3. A. C. RICHARDS will read the List of Vice-Presidents and Secretaries.

4. PELATIAH PERIT, Chairman, will address the Meeting.

5. CHARLES H. RUSSELL will read the ADDRESS adopted by the Convention of Committees.

6. SAMUEL D. BABCOCK will read the RESOLUTIONS adopted by the Convention of Committees.

7. MUSIC—Volunteer Chorus, by HENRY CAMP and FRIENDS,— Star-Spangled Banner.

8. Rev. FRANCIS VINTON will address the Meeting.

9. MUSIC—Volunteer Songs—God Speed the Right.

10. CHARLES P. DALY will address the Meeting.

11. MUSIC—Hail Columbia.

12. DAVID S. CODDINGTON will address the Meeting.

Mr. PROSPER M. WETMORE called the meeting to order, read the call for the meeting, and also the following letter from Mr. PELATIAH PERIT, who had been designated by the Committee of arrangements to preside over the stand.

LETTER OF P. PERIT.

NEW HAVEN, *July* 14*th*, 1862.

John A. Stevens, Jr., Esq., Secretary Chamber of Commerce, N. Y.:

MY DEAR SIR,—I have been favored to-day with your telegraphic note of this date informing me that I have been appointed to preside at the stand of the Chamber of Commerce, at the public meeting to be held to-morrow.

Having been confined to my bed by sickness since my return from New-York, I am quite unable to proceed to the city, and shall thus be prevented from taking part in the great demonstration.

That the meeting will be large and enthusiastic, I cannot doubt, and I trust it will be as powerful in its influence for good as was that which followed the attack on Sumter.

I shall be present with you in feeling though not in person.

Very truly, yours,
P. PERIT.

Mr. WETMORE nominated for Chairman Mr. A. A. LOW, second Vice-President of the Chamber of Commerce, who was unanimously elected.

Mr. A. C. RICHARDS read the list of Vice-Presidents and Secretaries which had been prepared by the Committee, and which was adopted with unanimity.

ADDRESS OF A. A. LOW, ESQ.

FELLOW-CITIZENS,—I share with you in your regret that the much respected gentleman, who was expected to preside over this meeting, is prevented by illness from being present. The honor naturally belonged to one who has, so often, by his cheering presence, imparted grace and dignity to our public gatherings; and I know with what pleasure he has answered every expectation when the interests of this community have been involved.

In the absence of Mr. PERIT, to whom I have just referred, and in the absence of the first Vice-President of the Chamber of Commerce, it devolves upon me, in obedience to your vote, to announce the object of this meeting.

Indeed, it needs no announcement. There is but one call that brings together men of all parties, of all professions, and of every name. It is the call of our country. The existing emergency is too well understood to require any labored explanations. Your response to the summons which has brought you here has been too hearty and enthusiastic to warrant a passionate appeal to your patriotism.

In this great metropolis of the Union, in this Square, consecrated to the Union, by the great pledges recorded here a year ago in April, it is especially meet that, at this critical juncture, men of all parties should assemble once more and unite in a fresh resolve to support the Constitution and the Union; to sustain the Chief Executive of the nation; to give a new impulse to the popular mind; to manifest by word and by deed an unalterable determination to sustain the great cause for which such sacrifices have been made—for which so much blood has been shed.

For more than a year one great burden has rested upon every loyal heart. Your most anxious thoughts for yourselves and for your children have centered upon our country, convulsed by civil war, and still doomed to suffer. Your brightest hopes, your most glorious anticipations have all been directed to the re-establishment of this great Republic, in its full and magnificent proportions. For this, brave men have fought, and good men have prayed.

Through all discouragements, and through all reverses, this has been the undeviating purpose, the unfaltering trust of good and true men. To see the people of the United States, from North to South and East to West, bound together once more by a common interest and a common love in our vast brotherhood, has been the paramount desire, the ardent prayer of every true patriot.

Touch your throbbing hearts, and tell me if this be not so; if, through all the anxious and eventful scenes of our great national struggle, superior to every fear, one hope has not predominated all other hopes—the ever ardent aspiration that our country may survive its fiery trial—may soon issue forth triumphantly, "both purified and glorified!" That this last experiment of man to found and sustain a Republican government, whose standard is the symbol of civil and religious freedom, may become an unquestioned success; and that these United States, increasing in number and growing in grandeur, may continue to be the asylum of the oppressed, the admiration of all lovers of liberty, the fear of all the foes of freedom throughout the world.

During the great crisis which has so tasked the energies of the whole country, the city of New-York has poured forth in unmeasured flow her money and her men, answering every requisition with an unstinted hand. True to the inspirations of her extended commerce, her contributions to the finances of the country have been generous and bountiful. The merchants of this city know too well the value of free and uninterrupted intercourse with every section of the Union, of open ports and navigable rivers, to be indifferent to the issues of this great controversy, did not a more worthy patriotism prompt to the largest sacrifices for the attainment of the noblest ends.

Your presence here to-day, in answer to the call, so hastily promulgated, shows that you are alive to the importance of the crisis; that nothing will be wanting on your part which may be asked of loyal and intelligent men that is conducive to an honorable adjustment of our National difficulties; that you appreciate the magnitude of the effort still to be made; and that you are prepared for every sacrifice that duty enjoins, that patriotism dictates.

The Committee of Arrangements have caused an Address to be prepared, which will now be read to you; and a series of Resolutions will be submitted for your consideration.

I shall presently have the honor of introducing several distinguished citizens, who have been invited to enforce these resolutions by their eloquent words.

Mr. SAMUEL SLOAN read the Address adopted by the Convention of Committees, which was received with great applause.

Mr. A. C. RICHARDS read the Resolutions adopted by the Convention of Committees which were accepted with cheers.

JUDGE DALY'S ADDRESS.

The Chairman then introduced Hon. CHARLES P. DALY, First Judge of the Common Pleas, who was received with applause. He said:—

When two parts of a great nation have divided, and are arrayed in open war against each other, it is a waste of time to dwell upon the causes that have produced it. Having thrown all other considerations aside, and grappled together in mortal strife, nothing remains then but to determine which of the two will be compelled to yield. [Cheers.] There was a time when mediation and compromise were possible. It has passed, and it is of no consequence now who are responsible for the neglect or opposition by which that opportunity was lost. He that supposes that the South would listen to any terms of settlement now, except such as it is impossible for the North to grant, is a political dreamer. Nothing can be done now except what is done by military means. The South has taken its position, and it will not recede from it unless it is compelled to. Whatever Union sentiment may have existed there, it is crushed out, and there is nothing apparent there now but sympathetic unanimity and a dogged determination to persist in the course they have taken. Whatever doubt, hesitation or difference of opinion may have prevailed at first, the sentiment is now universal that they have gone so far that they cannot go back; that they must now go on, whatever may be the consequence or the sacrifice. Everything with them, then, is reduced to a question of endurance, and the sooner we wake up to the consciousness of this state of facts, the more fully will we comprehend our own position and the obligations and duties that are imposed upon us. [Cheers.] Leaving out of view the political differences which may have incited and led to this war, what is it that the South have determined with such great unanimity to do, and which the North, with equal unanimity, have determined to resist? Constituting but little more than one third of the population of the whole country, the inhabitants of the Southern States have determined to seize the largest part of our territory, geographically; to appropriate to themselves nearly the whole of our sea-coast, and the mouths of nearly all our principal rivers—and construct out of it a foreign nation. Of the eighty-four rivers which, descending through a common territory, find their way to the sea and serve as the great outlets of the industry and commerce of the whole people, they modestly propose to take to themselves the possession and control of seventy-two, including the largest and most important; leaving to us but the number of twelve, watering that comparatively small strip of territory extending from the Hudson River to the northern boundary of Maine. [Groans.] They propose to cut us off from those elements of national existence determined by the curvature of mountain forms and by the course of rivers, and leave us a territory so irregular and so badly adjusted in respect to its dependent parts, as to make it impossible for us to keep it together as a nation. Look at the political boundaries of the nations upon the map of the globe, and not one will be found with a territory so disjointed and fragmentary as the one that would then be left us. If a foreign nation undertook to do this, we would resist to the last drop of our blood; and does it make any difference that those who are seeking to accomplish it, have hitherto been a part of ourselves, and proffer to us in the future nothing but vows of eternal hate? [Applause.] After eighty-six years of existence as one government and one people, eight millions rise up and say to twenty millions, "We will take the largest part of this country for ourselves, and you must accept what we think proper to leave you; we are the better born, the nobler race, the aristocracy; we do not choose to labor ourselves, we prefer to have a servile class to labor for us, and therefore have no sympathy with the trading spirit by which you have increased and multiplied, nor with the mechanical, manufacturing and various industrial pursuits to which you are devoted." [Groans.] They say to us, "There has never been such a thing as the American nation; it has been only a mere partnership of sovereign states which any one might dissolve at its pleasure. We have respectively dissolved it, and in the partition of the partnership effects we have made our own adjustment, taken what has pleased us, and left to you what we thought proper." To submit to this is to allow the weaker to dictate to the stronger—[cries of "Never"]—to allow the eight millions of the South to prescribe to the twenty millions of the North what shall be their future position. The man who was born in a Northern State, or who became a citizen by adoption, is as much a citizen of South Carolina as those who were born or who dwell there. [Cheers.] And neither their Southern doctrine of State rights, nor their rebellious attempt at exclusiveness, can deprive him of it. To submit to the designs of the South, is to consent to national annihilation. It is to consent, in a national point of view, to take territorially an inferior and subordinate position; to take a territory so placed geographically, that its dismemberment, the breaking of it up into several parts, must be the inevitable consequence. The question, then, is not whether we shall conquer the South, but whether the South shall conquer us. [Cheers.] It is whether the present aristocracy of the Southern States, and their retainers, shall deprive the intelligent and industrious masses of the North of a territory, the joint possession of which they have equally inherited, and which is essential to the unfettered exercise of their industry, and to their full development as a nation. It is this which gives to this contest the character of a mortal struggle, in which neither will yield unless compelled to do so by the superior military prowess of the other. [Applause.] It is not like other civil wars—a struggle between two classes of society, living together, where the one seeks to get the mastery over the other and establish a form of government; but it is one part of a country enjoying in every respect the same political privileges which insists upon breaking off territorially, and which for that purpose has arrayed itself in open war against the other. [Cheers.] The thing which most nearly resembles it is the division of the once compact Republic of Colombia into the now insignificant States of Ecuador, New Grenada and Venezuela, with the fruitful lesson which that furnishes in the miserable state of anarchy now prevailing in these distracted and wretched countries. We have scarcely yet risen in the North to the full consciousness of the magnitude of the struggle in which we are engaged. We have not fully comprehended the momentous consequences which are involved and the vital and disastrous effects upon us if we fail to succeed.

In this struggle, which to us is for existence, we have a task upon us equivalent to the conquering of a nation. [Cheers.] We have from the beginning undervalued the capacity and power of resistance on the part of the South, and have men now in Congress, who believe that the South is to be conquered by the enactment of laws—[laughter and cheers]—Congressional doctors ignorant enough to think that an armed rebellion of eight millions of people can be put down by the passage of statutes. We have not realized the extent of resources that is demanded—of money, of men, and of the material of war. As a peaceful people, suddenly roused up, we have displayed extraordinary energy, and in so short a space of time have put forth an extent of naval and military strength almost incredible. [Cheers.] But great as has been our effort, that of the South has been greater. She has drafted the whole of her available population, determined to overmatch us by the promptitude with which she has brought troops into the field. She is said to have two hundred and twenty thousand men now at Richmond, while we have not half that number. She has made a last great effort; and, should we pause here, it will be, on her part, a successful one. We will be beaten, humiliated and disgraced. All that we have hitherto done will have gone for nothing, and we will retire from the contest with a contracted territory and a gigantic load of debt, which of itself will be a reason for one part of the country to shift it off upon the other by acts of dismemberment and separation. To avert these calamities, a call is made by the Government upon the country for three hundred thousand men; and if that call is promptly responded to, the suppression of the rebellion will be but a question of time. [Cheers.] It will soon be seen whether our people are, or are not, equal to the great emergency which now calls upon them to act. If they fail in this crisis, then the South are, as they have claimed to be, our masters. They will triumph in the consciousness that they have chafed into submission those artisans, tradesmen and laborers of the North. We are masters upon the water, but on the land the heart of this rebellion has not yet been reached, and it will not be unless this levy is raised. If this call is responded to, and three hundred thousand men rapidly put in the field we shall be armed in a double sense:—First, it will secure us against foreign intervention—[loud cheers]; and, secondly, we shall accomplish what we undertook to do when we first rose to the defence of our government and our flag. The season, being the time of harvest, is not a propitious one, and if, from that or any other cause, this force cannot be raised by volunteering in time to meet the present pressing emergencies of the government, I can see no good reason why a draft should not at once be made. [Loud and general expression of approbation.] Our enemies have resorted to it, and it is now the chief source of their strength. The government of Europe which most nearly resembles our own—the republic of Switzerland—was placed a few years ago in a situation exactly like ours. The southern cantons undertook to break off and establish a confederate government by themselves. The northern cantons, constituting, as we do, the majority of the population, raised an army and crushed the rebellion. The plan which they resorted to, and which proved eminently successful, was to draft the whole of the requisite force in the very beginning. It brought into the army men of all ranks and conditions, making it a high-toned, intelligent and patriotic body. While our system of volunteering is enormously expensive, the measure adopted by the republic of Switzerland was economical and brought together a devoted, disinterested and patriotic body of men. It is at least fair and just in its operation, as it casts the duty of defending the government equally upon all classes—[cheers]—and if the necessity should exist I do not see why we should hesitate to resort to it. The man who is not willing to defend a free and liberal government like this, when the lot is cast upon him, is unfit to live under it and enjoy its blessings. [Loud applause.] Our national existence, then, depends upon our obtaining the three hundred thousand men. To that every other consideration is subordinate. Like Aaron's rod, it swallows up every other, and the whole energies of the people and of the Government must be devoted to it. But the men now called to come forth to the rescue of the nation, have a right to demand that they shall be led by generals, and not by politicians in uniform; and we, men of all parties assembled here to-day in this mighty gathering of the intelligence and patriotism of the masses of this great metropolis, have a right to call upon our temporary rulers at Washington to imitate the example which is here set them of unity, of public spirit and patriotism, [cheers]; to leave off the discussion of measures upon which we are a divided people, and think only of the preservation of the country in this pressing crisis. Let them bear in mind that they are not as great men as they suppose themselves to be, and learn something of that fine element of character—humility. Let them remember that more than two thirds of the men composing the army of the Union are opposed to them politically, and, above all, let the civilians in Washington give up directing and controlling the operations of generals in the field. [Loud cheers.] The Archduke Charles was but little inferior in military genius to Napoleon, and with the superior numbers at his command might have been more than a match for his great adversary, had not his operations in the field been controlled by the Aulic Council sitting at Vienna. To this body every unemployed general and intrusive civilian, as at Washington, had access, and, ignorant of the changes and vicissitudes which attend a campaign, this Council baffled the best laid plans of the Archduke by controlling his opinion and prescribing beforehand what the movement of the armies should be; and had not Wellington, in the war of the Peninsula, openly disregarded the suggestions, and even orders, that came to him from London, the British arms would never have triumphed over the generals of Napoleon. [Cheers.] No general under heaven can accomplish anything if, in addition to the enemy in front, he has also to fight against an army of detractors and advisers in his rear. [Prolonged applause.] If he is incompetent, take the responsibility and remove him; but while he is in command let him command. We can raise the three hundred thousand men; but if the spirit of meddlesome interference at Washington, controlling the operations of generals in the field, does not meet the contempt it deserves in the indignant rebuke of our whole people, then our energies will be wasted again, and in the fullness of national calamity we will be left but to lament over the madness and folly of our temporary rulers. [Loud applause.]

Three cheers were given for Judge DALY.

SPEECH OF HON. DAVID S. CODDINGTON.

Hon. D. S. CODDINGTON was the next speaker. He was greeted with applause, and said :—

FELLOW-CITIZENS,—In this hour of alienation, tumult, and disaster, no man, however humble, has a right to sit still when the nation has sprung to its feet, and the Union lies bleeding upon its back. [Cheers.]

We have come here in the darkest hour of National existence to declare before the world that the unity and nationality of America shall not be dissolved, either in the swamps of the Chickahominy or the Council Chambers of Paris or London. [Great applause.] We are all, under moral martial law, now bound to obey every draft upon the brain, the heart, the purse, and the life, to serve a Government, whose authority has dropped upon us with the gentleness of a flower, and yet shielded us with the strength of a giant. We may have our weaknesses, and these weaknesses may serve to point an English sneer, or round a Southern taunt ; but they never yet have succeeded in vitiating the grander points of our National character, neither have they, for one moment, obstructed the beneficent action of our hitherto unassailable institutions. [Cheers.]

If secession is right, then all order, all regulated society, is wrong. If secession cannot be put down without war, then war is the highest duty and best business of the American citizen—more profitable than merchandise, more beautiful than poetry, and, for the time being, as sacred as the ministry itself. True, we may fail sometimes ; so do all business and sciences until experience teaches them. By degrees we shall learn the art of blood, and mayhap the foe will find the Yankee shop-boy an efficient chronic portable slaughter-house. So far we have fought half tiger and half brother. No half man accomplishes much. We must be all tiger now, that we may be all brothers by and by. [Laughter and applause.]

If fevers and blunders have wasted the strength and tampered with the glory of our armies, the beautiful enthusiasm of this day's proceedings illustrates how heartily and abundantly we try to redeem our errors and relieve our heroes. Was it not a sublime spectacle to see the President of the United States pouring the balm of his sympathizing Presidential presence into the serried ranks of the wearied army of the Potomac--ABRAHAM LINCOLN confronting GEO. B. MCCLELLAN? [Loud cheers for McClellan.] The embodied representative of the National authority shaking hands with the genius of American safety--the great rail-splitter reproaching the railers against the noble army and its gifted chieftain.

When ABRAHAM LINCOLN was nominated, I laughed at the convention; when he was elected, I trembled for the country; but since he has been inaugurated, I have learned to love and honor the man who has so faithfully wielded the National resources. [Great applause.] When the South struck at the President, they fired at a man in the stocks, cooped up in judicial decisions, bound down by legislative restrictions, warned away from all philanthropic mischief by the wholesome hostility of an adverse popular vote. They found him in quiet, helpless, party paralysis, and only left him an aroused, wounded, angry National giant, with all the resources of all parties at his command.

The South sneered at our poor, under-fed, over-worked soldiers, who fled from Bull Run; but now the world laughs at a whole community who ran away from a shadow. Our soldiers left a few arms and knapsacks on the field, while they threw away long years of happiness and prosperity. Daily are we taunted with their superiority in arms and birth. They claim WASHINGTON, as if their deeds had made him. Out of the 200,000 troops who fought in the War of the Revolution, the South did not furnish 20,000. But for the North, WASHINGTON would have gone down to posterity with a halter around his neck. It was Northern hands that moulded his Virginia clay into an immortal statue. [Sensation.]

Compared with our solid successes, what have the South achieved in this war? Two or three land checks and one steam fright. [Laughter.] The ghost of the *Merrimac* will haunt the nation for centuries. By diverting the base of operations from the James River, it has cost us $100,-000,000. That sum would have built us 300 *Monitors*, which would have blockaded all intervention.

The march of events now means the march of armies. The progress of our institutions depends at last upon the speed of our bullets; when they rain the Union is safe, when they slacken the Union reels. War is a cruel alternative, but not more so than a peace which removes from danger without relieving us of disgrace, disorder, and disintegration. We want not lamentation over this war, but enlistments in the war. Let us shed no tears but volunteers. [Great laughter.] We cannot succeed in this gigantic war until all classes are worked up to the thrusting point.

There must be a fighting man from every family and every calling; a fighting lawyer, a fighting doctor, a fighting priest, ay, and a fighting dandy. Now is the time for white kids to redeem themselves. Now is the time for all that army of fashionable loungers who have been growling all their lives for lack of opportunity. Now is the time for them to rise, strike and be immortal. ["Good, good."] While the South have sent a thousand men to battle, we have sent a hundred. While they have mounted science to lead on their armies to victory, we have too often skipped experience and thrust politics on horseback to save the country. Twenty-three millions of people are tired of being told that they are outwitted because they are outnumbered. [Cheers.] If we fall now we will be the oddest ruin on record. Rome was four hundred years dying of her own corruptions. We, instead of being enervated by luxury or discomfited by invasion, go down with all our strength and all our wealth, and all our wits about us. [Applause.] Destroyed by a remark, our great light blown out by the passionate breath of partisan oratory. [Great applause.] I, for one, can never believe in such a death. The ablest sword of the age is hanging by our side. The heaviest purse on the Continent is in our pocket; the noblest cause for which man can draw his brother's blood, calls him to the battle-field, and if we wait patiently and act vigorously the greatest victory of modern times is in our grasp— the victory of the Republic over itself, the victory of democrat virtues over aristocrat vices, the victory of law, order, and Government over disunion, distraction, conflagration, and damnation. [Long applause.]

On conclusion of the honorable gentleman's remarks, three cheers were proposed for Mr. CODDINGTON, which were vociferously responded to.

The Chairman, A. A. LOW, Esq., said :—

FELLOW-CITIZENS,—We have here the Rev. Dr. FRANCIS VINTON. He did not intend to speak; but if there be a man from whom we have a right to expect a word, it is he. He belongs to a family, (as many of you know,) who have not only given their voice and their service, but their blood, to the country. He himself, though now a clergyman of one of our principal churches—old Trinity—is a West Pointer, and has served in the United States Army through one war. His nephew commands the 43d New-York Volunteers in the Army of the Potomac. A brother is the distinguished Deputy Quartermaster-General of the Army in this city; and another brother, father of the Colonel of the 43d, died while in command of the trenches before Vera Cruz. [Cheers and cries, "Let us hear him."] I will ask the Rev. Doctor to say a few words to us [Cheers.]

Dr. Vinton then came forward and spoke, substantially, as follows :—

SPEECH OF REV. DR. FRANCIS VINTON.

FELLOW-CITIZENS,—I could not, after listening to such a call as that which I have just heard, remain silent and decline to lift my voice to speak to you. This war was not begun by us. When Major Anderson was summoned to surrender Fort Sumter to the rebels, he refused, but added, in an unofficial way, that in three days he would be starved out, and compelled to evacuate the fort. When his reply, official and unofficial, was telegraphed to Montgomery, the lightning flashed across the wires this response from the Confederate Government, "Open fire at once." Those rebel guns inaugurated the war against the Flag and the Constitution and the Union of the United States.

We have been, ever since, waging a defensive war—a war to defend, to protect and to maintain the Union and Constitution of our country, and thus to preserve our life as a nation.

At this particular crisis, the war has become a question of honor or dishonor, of liberty or slavery, of death or of life, to you and your children.

I waive all debate as to foregone points of policy or of party, of mistake, of fraud, and whatever things soever have irritated and divided the Free States, and I say that a crisis is upon us, when every patriot, whether he be father or mother, son or daughter, must lay the offering of his dearest possession upon the altar, in obedience to the command of God and of the State. Let our Isaac be ever so closely knit to our hearts and our hopes, we must be the faithful Abraham to give him up in sacrifice. [Cheers.]

I have served our country in her army for ten years, and I speak to you as a military man. And I tell you that we have not lost an equal battle in this whole war; even at Bull Run, we beat the army opposed to us. Beauregard, in his official report of that battle, says to Davis, that he had reluctantly given orders to retreat—that when he saw the columns approaching in his rear, he did not know whether they belonged to Patterson or to Johnson; but when he found that they were reinforcements, and not opponents, then he began to hope for victory.

In every action since Bull Run (except, perhaps, Ball's Bluff) the loyal army of the United States has conquered the rebels, in fair fight and often against odds, causing them to evacuate and "skedaddle" after their first *élan* and onslaught. In proof of this, look at Bowling Green and Corinth, and the previous battles which delivered Missouri; look at the evacuation of Columbus, of Manassas, of Yorktown, of Norfolk, and the defeat at Williamsburg, to say nothing of what our army and navy combined, have accomplished at Port Royal, and Fort Donelson and New Orleans.

But what chiefly demonstrates the superiority of the Union forces over the rebels, are the late series of victories of McClellan [cheers] in his march from the Pamunkey to the James River, in the last week of June and the first two days of July.

McClellan conquered the rebels in seven successive battles on seven successive days; wherever he encountered the rebels he overthrew them, and is nearer Richmond now than ever he was before. [Cheers.] With the strong right arm of the country supporting him on James River—the navy—I say he is nearer to Richmond than ever. Though in the change of front to the new base of operations on James River, our army lost ten thousand men, yet the enemy lost (as they confess) thirty thousand; while we succeeded, in that manœuvre, in concentrating the power of our forces, and the rebels were defeated in their attempt to prevent it.

Fellow-citizens, there are some among us who echo the rebels' boast, and misname McClellan's change of front, a *retreat*, and his casualties, a *defeat*. Nothing, in a military point of view, is more false than this aspect of the late battles before Richmond. What are the facts of the case? The James River is the natural avenue to Richmond; McClellan could not advance on that route while Norfolk was in possession of the rebels, and while the iron-clad *Merrimac* blockaded the mouth of the James River. When Norfolk was taken and the *Merrimac* was destroyed, and our gun-boats had reached City Point, it was the true policy of McClellan to join the gun-boats, and unite our naval and military forces.

McClellan, as early as Friday, in the third week of June, gave orders to remove the stores from the White House and the York River, round to the James. And it was done effectually, and without interruption or loss, by the following Tuesday. On Tuesday he moved his army; it was attacked, and the attack was repulsed; fresh hordes of the fugitives of Beauregard with the veterans of Johnson and Lee repeated the assaults on Wednesday, and Thursday, and Friday, and Saturday and Sunday, and each onslaught was repelled: on Monday, the advance of our army reached the James River, driving before them three thousand head of cattle and dragging their siege guns through the swamps of the Chickahominy, without the loss of a hoof or the abandonment of a gun. The dead and the wounded were necessarily left behind, and several fieldpieces (twenty-five in number) were disabled and captured. Prisoners were taken and provisions in baggage wagons were captured. This was all our damage, though it was fearful and saddening.

On Monday the rebels renewed the fight on the rear-guard, and were again repulsed with loss of whole brigades of rebel prisoners and of twenty-six of their guns. On Tuesday the reserve of the enemy marched from Richmond, fresh and untired, with the expectation of getting into the rear of our exhausted troops; but they were met and held until our gun-boats, the *Galena* and the *Monitor*, opened a terrific fire, which sent the frightened rebels hurly skurly back to Richmond. Thus ended the foiled attempts to outgeneral McClellan. [Cheers.] Thus terminated the rebel efforts to beat our brave soldiers of the Army of the Potomac. [Cheers.] It is worth noticing, that the correspondent of the New-York *Tribune* relates that he was on board of the *Galena* when McClellan arrived on board from a skiff, and posted the gun-boat by his own directions to her commander; that then he went aboard of the *Monitor*, and pointed out the proper position for that champion to take. [Cheers.] It was a spectacle like that of Perry passing from the Lawrence to the Niagara, and plucking victory from a competent foe by the force of mind and valor. It was the shots from these, his naval coadjutors, which gave the finishing blow to the rebels in their last assault, and sent them back to their rebel capital. [Cheers for McClellan.]

Now, fellow-citizens, does all this wear the aspect of McClellan's defeat, or of McClellan's victories? The rebels were foiled, and the Union Army was successful. And I claim the series of victories, costly as they were, to McClellan and his army, and so will history record her judgment. Why, let me put the case in a familiar way: suppose that you were going over the ferry to Brooklyn, where two or three rowdies encountered you, and swore that you should not go; they attack you, and you knock them down, one after another, and go on your way, and reach the other side as you intended. Who conquered? Who got the victory? Will you say that you were defeated, because your clothes were torn and your nose bloody, or even if your arm were broken and your purse gone?

These are the casualties of the occasion. You were not the conquered, but the victors. This is a plain and homely, but true illustration, of the seven days' battle of McClellan. The enemy assailed him three to one, and he drove them off. [Cheers.] Fellow-citizens, I knew most of the leaders of this rebellion at West Point and in the army. And among them are men, whom, before the rebellion, I have known as gentlemen; but the Bible says, that " Rebellion is as witchcraft ;" Samuel uttered this divine condemnation to Saul, and when Saul became a rebel, his very nature was, as by witchcraft, changed, and so now again, has this rebellion changed those whom I once recognized as friends and gentlemen. They have become our foes, and, in their attempts to destroy the Constitution and Union and Government of the United States, they would be our murderers, like Saul against David. They would kill us or make us vassals. Shall they do this, or shall every traitor to the Constitution be made to feel the authority and power of the Government of the United States? The Army of the Potomac must be recruited and reinforced. The President has called for 300,000 loyal soldiers. Shall we go to the army or stay at home? Who will not offer himself as a champion or a martyr for his country, in this crisis of constitutional liberty? Who will not enlist when victory or death are the issues? Who will not go to the altar, like Isaac, to be priest or sacrifice, as God may appoint, and win an imperishable name on the muster-roll of a nation's heroes? Let the example of Mr. Seward's son be an example to us. *The Secretary of State, in his letter just now read, tells you that he has offered his youngest son to the service of his country, as a private in one of the military organizations of New York.* [Prolonged and enthusiastic applause.]

SPEECH OF PETER COOPER.

In response to a call from the Meeting, PETER COOPER came forward and said :—

FELLOW-CITIZENS,—I can assure you that nothing could give me greater pleasure than to be able to say a word, if possible, that would awake the slumbering energies of the nation to the magnitude of the war in which we are engaged. [Cheers.] We are contending with an enemy not only determined on our destruction as a nation, but an enemy that is determined to build on our ruins a government with all its power devoted to maintain, extend, and perpetuate a system in itself revolting to all the best feelings of humanity. An institution that enables thousands to sell their own children into hopeless bondage. [A voice—" That's so! I have seen it."] Shall it succeed? [Cries of " No! No!"] You say no, and I unite with you and say *no*, also. We cannot allow it to succeed. We should spend our lives, our property and leave the land a desolation before such an institution should triumph over the free people of this country. [Applause.]

I know, my friends, that will be the feeling when the people wake up to the importance of the present occasion ; and I believe the time has now come that we begin to see that thousands, nay millions, are sighing to help us, but are afraid because they say we are fighting to restore an institution that will keep them in perpetual bondage.

I trust the day has come when we shall unbind the heavy burdens and let the captives go free—when we shall meet these men who are ready to unite and aid us, and give us the help we need. [Cheers.] A help that will take from the rebels the power on which they depend for digging their trenches, plowing their fields, raising their crops, and leaving them leisure to play upon us the game of war. Shall it be so any longer? I trust it shall not. Let us unite and do what we can to convince the people of the South, that their best interests call for the freedom of their slaves, and not only of their slaves, but the freedom of the white people of the South from the terrible thralldom, the terrible dependence they are in, when they allow themselves to rely on a coerced and uncompensated labor. [Cheers.] Let us unite in an effort to sustain the Government by every means in our power, and get the army built up in the shortest possible time, with the best men and arms that can be found. [Enthusiastic applause.]

The proceedings at this stand were then closed.

OFFICERS.

STAND No. 3.

Under charge of Committee of Arrangements,
PETER MITCHELL,   CHARLES GOULD.

President.

HAMILTON FISH, *President of Union Defence Committee.*

Vice-Presidents.

William B. Astor,
Moses H. Grinnell,
William C. Bryant,
Luther Bradish,
James Lenox,
Joseph Sampson,
Charles H. Marshall,
George Bancroft,
Robert Ray,
Samuel B. Ruggles,
Peter Cooper,
C. R. Robert,
Henry W. Bellows,
Merritt Trimble,
James W. Beekman,
Alexander T. Stewart,
Richard M. Blatchford,
Thomas Tileston,
George T. Adee,
John Cotton Smith,
Frederic Depeyster,
Cyrus Curtiss,
William Aymar,
Henry L. Pierson,
F. S. Winston,
Adrian Iselin,
George T. Strong,
James L. Morris,
Benj. D. Silliman,
Frederick G. Foster,
William A. Darling,
Charles A. Heckscher,
Japhet Bishop,
Hugo Wesendonck,
A. C. Richards,
Charles B. Hoffman,

Lorillard Spencer,
George S. Robbins,
James Punnett,
William Post,
A. L. Robertson,
William Barton,
Richard Warren,
Otis D. Swan,
Elias Wade, Jr.,
O. D. F. Grant,
Theodore Polhemus,
Anthony S. Hope,
William Allen Butler,
Edward A. Bibby,
Jacob Hayes,
William F. Cary,
James Renwick,
Samuel M. Fox,
J. Butler Wright,
Frederick Sheldon,
Caleb Barstow,
Frederick Prime,
J. B. Giraud Foster,
James B. Murray,
Alexander Hamilton,
Wm. P. Esterbrook,
Alexander S. Leonard,
John Trenor,
William Black,
Edmund Schermerhorn,
David S. Coddington,
George Donalson,
Franklin H. Delano,
Jonathan Thorne,
John Sedgwick,
Robert J. Livingston,

Philetus H. Holt,
Samuel T. Bridgham,
Thomas M. Adriance,
P. Remsen Strong,
Isaac Green Pearson,
Adam Norrie,
John Ward,
William C. Rhinelander,
Israel Corse,
George W. Blunt,
Francis B. Nicol,
Daniel H. Turner,

Henry Drisler,
Wickham Hoffman,
Albert R. Gallatin,
Horace Green,
Howard Potter,
Lorenzo Draper,
James A. Briggs,
James M. Cross,
Henry A. Smythe,
Thomas Addis Emmet,
Herman R. LeRoy,
C. E. Detmold.

Secretaries.

Frank Moore,
John H. White,
Sheppard Gandy,
George W. Ogston,
Samuel Blatchford,
James F. Ruggles,
Frank W. Ballard,
John Nesbitt,
Robert Cutting,
William S. Chamberlain,
William Bibby
Oliver King,
Samuel Curtis,

Henry P. Benkard,
Charles C. Nott,
Charles Neilson,
J. Winthrop Chanler,
William J. Emmet,
Henry A. Oakley,
Charles Goodhue,
George B. Waldron,
Elliot F. Shepard,
Robert Benson, Jr.,
Nathaniel Prime,
William Rhinelander.

PROGRAMME OF PROCEEDINGS.

STAND No. 3.

SALUTES OF ARTILLERY BY ANTHON LIGHT BATTERY and by the WORKMEN employed by HENRY BREWSTER & Co.

1. MUSIC—Grand March by

2. PETER MITCHELL will call the meeting to order, read the call of the meeting, and conduct HAMILTON FISH to the chair.

3. W. E. DODGE will read the list of Vice-Presidents and Secretaries.

4. HAMILTON FISH, Chairman, will address the meeting.

5. CHARLES GOULD will read the ADDRESS adopted by the Convention of Committees.

6. PETER MITCHELL will read the RESOLUTIONS adopted by the Convention of Committees.

7. MUSIC.

8. ETHAN ALLEN will deliver an Address.

9. MUSIC.

10. R. D. HITCHCOCK will deliver an address.

11. MUSIC.

12. JOHN A. KING.

13. MUSIC.

In the absence of HAMILTON FISH, who had been designated to preside over this stand, CHARLES GOULD, of the Committee of Arrangements, was called to the Chair.

Mr. GEORGE W. BLUNT read the Address. The Resolutions were read by Alderman MITCHELL, and adopted unanimously.

Weigand's band having given the "Star-Spangled Banner," the first speaker introduced was Mr. ETHAN ALLEN, Assistant U. S. District Attorney, who spoke as follows:—

MR. ETHAN ALLEN'S SPEECH.

FELLOW-CITIZENS OF NEW-YORK,—Once more the tocsin sounds to arms, and freemen rally to the call. It is now nearly a century ago that mass meetings of our fathers were held in this city, to devise ways and means for the defence of that very flag, which to-day is given to the winds of Heaven, beaming defiance from every star. Fired then with the same spirit of freedom that kindles on this spot to-day, for the time throwing aside the habiliments of peace, our fathers armed themselves for vengeance and for war. The *history* of that war, go read it in the hearts of the American people; the *trials* and *struggles* of that war, mark them in the tear-drop which the very allusion calls to every eye; the *blessings* of that war, count them in the gorgeous temples of trade that rise everywhere around you; the *wisdom* of that war, and the promised *perpetuity of its triumphs*, behold the one in our unexampled national prosperity, and the other in the impulses that like an electric flash bind heart to heart throughout this vast assemblage in the firm resolve, that, cost what it may, rebellion shall go down. [Loud applause.]

Again the American people are assembled in mass meetings throughout the nation, while the States once more rock in the throes of a revolution. Once more the cry to arms reverberates throughout the land; but this time we war against domestic foes. Treason has raised its black flag near the tomb of Washington, and the Union of our States hangs her fate upon the bayonet and the sword. Accursed be the hand that would not use the bayonet—blighted be the arm that would not wield the sword in such a cause! Everything that the American citizen holds dear hangs upon the issue of this contest. Our national honor and reputation demand that rebellion shall not triumph on our soil. In the name of our heroic dead, in the name of our numberless victories upon the battle-field, in the name of our thousand peaceful triumphs, in the name of our unexampled national prosperity, our Union must and shall be preserved. [Enthusiastic cheers.]

Our peaceful triumphs! These are really the important victories which we should be jealous to guard. They are worth fighting for; they are worth dying for. They are fostered and multiplied under the protection of the "Union;" otherwise the term "Union" were but empty sound. Let others recount their marshal glories: they shall be eclipsed by the charity and the grace of the triumphs which have been achieved in peace. "Peace hath her victories, not less renowned than War," and the hard-earned fruits of these victories rebellion shall not take from us. [Cries of "No," "No," "Never."] Our peaceful triumphs! Who shall enumerate their value to the millions yet unborn? What nation, in so short a time, has won so many? On the land and on the sea, in the realms of science and in the world of art, we everywhere have gathered our honors, and have won our garlands. Upon the altars of the States they yet lie, fresh from the gathering, while their happy influences fill the land.

Of the importance and value of our thousand peaceful triumphs, time will permit me to mention only one, which is yet fresh in the memory of us all. It is now two years ago, when up the waters of the Potomac, toward the Capital, sailed the representatives of an empire till then shut out from intercourse with all Christian nations. In the eastern seas there lay an empire of islands, which hitherto had enjoyed no recognition in the Christian world, other than its name upon the map. No history, so far as we know, illumined it—no ancient time-mark told of its advance, step by step, in the march of improvement. There it had rested for thousands of years, wrapped in the mysteries of its own exclusiveness, "gloomy, dark, peculiar." It had been supposed to possess great power, and vague rumors had attributed to it, ingenious arts to us unknown. Against nearly all the world, for thousands of years, Japan had obstinately shut her doors. The wealth of the Christian world could not tempt her cupidity, the wonders of the Christian world could not excite her curiosity. There she lay, sullen and alone, the phenomenon of nations. England and France and the other powerful Governments of Europe had at various times tried to conquer this oriental exclusiveness, but the Portuguese only partially succeeded, while all the rest signally failed. At length, we, bearing at our masthead the glorious old stars and stripes, approach the mysterious portals, and seek an entrance. Not with cannon and implements of death do we demand admission, but appreciating the saying of Euripides, that

> "Resistless eloquence shall open
> The gates that steel exclude,"

we peacefully appeal to that sense of right, which is the "touch of nature that makes the whole world kin," and behold, the interdiction is removed, the doors of the mysterious empire fly open, and a new garland is woven, to crown the monument of our commercial conquests. [Loud applause.]

Who shall set limit to the gain that may follow this one victory of peace, if our Government be perpetuated so as to gather it for the generations? Who shall say, in an unbroken, undivided Union, that the opening of the ports of Japan shall not accomplish for the present era all that the Reformation, the art of printing, steam and the telegraph have done within the last three hundred years? New avenues of wealth are thrown open, new fields are to be occupied, arts new to us, doubtless, are to be studied and to be Americanized, and science, perhaps, from that arcana of nations, has revelations to make to us, equal to anything which we have ever learned before. Reciprocity bids us to extend whatever is valuable in our system of Government over this new convert to our national policy. Fifty millions of people there are to be enlightened; the printing-press is to catch the daily thought and stamp it upon the page; the magnetic wire must yet vibrate along her highways, and Niphon must be made to tremble to her centre, at each heart-beat of our ocean steamers, as they sweep through her waters or thunder round her island homes. [Cries of "Good," and applause.] All hail! all hail! to these children of the morning. All hail! all hail! to the great Republic of the West, that ushers them into life. From every age that has passed there comes a song of praise for the treaty that has been consummated. The buried masters of three thousand years start again to life, and march in solemn and in grand procession, before the eyes of these new-found empires. Homer with his songs, Greece with her arts, Rome with her legions, and America with her heroes, all come to them with the novelty and freshness of the newly-born. Wipe off the mould which time has gathered upon their tombs, and let them all come forth and answer, at the summons of new-born nations, that call them again to life; wrapped in the winding-sheet of eighteen centuries, the fishermen of Galilee tell to these strangers the story of the resurrection; clutching in their hands their dripping blades, the warriors recount their conquests; and joined at last in harmonious brotherhood, Copernicus, with bony fingers pointing upward, tells to Confucius his story of the stars. [Loud and enthusiastic cheering.]

Fellow-citizens, I have spoken of but one of our many peaceful triumphs. In this I may have been guilty of a digression from the subject which calls us together; but my aim has been to hold up our commercial conquests, gained while a law-abiding, united people, as eminently worthy of all the sacrifice of blood and treasure that we are called upon to make, in order to secure their legitimate fruits. It is really our numerous victories of peace, such as that of which I have spoken, that make us, as a nation, the wonder of the world. And let it be remembered that it was *freedom*, not *slavery*, that won these triumphs; it is *freedom* that must defend them. I appeal to you, shall all these peaceful honors of our people, shall all these hopes of the future, shall all these promised fruits from the struggles of the past, be swept away by the dissolution of the Union and the destruction of the Government? Forbid it, Almighty God! Rather perish, rather a thousand times perish, the cause of the rebellion, and over the ruins of Slavery let peace once more resume her sway, and let the cannon's lips grow cold. [Vociferous cheering.] *Delenda est Carthago*, said the old Roman patriot, when gloom settled upon his state; the rebellion must be crushed, with the same determination say we all to-day. [Applause.] The cannon that opened the fire upon Fort Sumter reverberated from the Penobscot to the Rocky Mountains, and has called the northern lion from his lair. Down with party, sect and class, and up with a sentiment of unanimity when our country calls to arms. Massachusetts, glorious old Massachusetts, first at the cradle of liberty in 1776, she will be the last at the grave, if fate intends that grave shall ever be. Again the "bones of her sons lie mingling and bleaching with the soil of every State from Maine to Georgia, and there they will lie forever." From her new-made graves she sends forth a constant prayer to Heaven; and let traitors tremble lest that prayer be answered. New-York must not be behind the Old Bay State. In the spirit world, Warren calls to Hamilton and Hamilton calls back to Warren, that hand in hand their mortal children go on together, to fame, to victory, or to the grave. The hosts of the Union are already marshaled in the field; but a call is made for more, and that call must not be in vain. [Cries of "No, no."] When the ranks are full, let us catch inspiration from the past, and under its influence go forth to conflict. Go call the rolls on Bemis Heights, on the plains of Monmouth, or at Yorktown, where the sheeted dead may rise as witness, and there propose to your legions the dissolution of this Union, and there receive their answer. Mad with frenzy, burning with indignation at the thought, all ablaze for vengeance upon the traitors, such will be the fury and impetuosity of the onset, that all opposition shall be swept before them, as the pigmy yields to the avalanche that comes tumbling, rumbling, thundering from its Alpine home. [Loud cheering.] Let us gather at the tomb of Washington, and invoke his spirit to direct us in the combat. Rising again incarnate from the tomb, in one hand holding the same old flag, blackened and begrimed by the smoke of a seven years' war, with the other hand he points us to the foe. Up and at them. Let patriotic fires thrill our very souls, while immortal spirits direct our way. One blow, deep, effectual and forever—one crushing blow upon rebellion, in the name of God, Washington and the Republic.

Three enthusiastic cheers were proposed and given with a will to Mr. ALLEN, as he concluded and took his seat.

"Hail Columbia," by the Band.

SPEECH OF REV. DR. HITCHCOCK.

The Rev. Dr. HITCHCOCK next took his place on the stand. He was rather heated when he rose, and took the opportunity of turning the same to advantage in his remarks, which were to the following effect:—

FELLOW-CITIZENS,—This sun is hot, but remember that it is not so hot as that sun which flames upon our brethren from a Virginia sky. Nor is that sun, that Virginia sun, half so hot as the fire of the artillery and musketry which blazes around those heroes who are now fighting for our cause, with this motto for their guide, "A glorious victory, or death." Nor is that fire of battle so hot as the fire of the hate of those who are now in rebellion against the Government of our country, who are shedding the life-blood of our brethren, against whom they are drawn up in battle array. My fellow-citizens of the great city of New-York, this meeting reminds me of the immense gathering which took place in this great commercial metropolis—the first great gathering of April, 1861. The month is an eventful one in our American history. It has its lights and its shadows, it is full of mingled opposites—at one time light, and at another time dark. It was in this month of April that we had our

Concord and our Lexington. It was also in this month of April that we had the attack upon and fall of Sumter. It was in this month of April that our brave soldiers were beset and brutally murdered in Baltimore. This meeting takes place in July, and July is also notable in our history as the month in which the Declaration of Independence was signed. April is a spring month, July is a harvest month. Fifteen months ago— in April, during the spring—we planted the seed of loyalty to the American Union, and it shall bring forth a glorious harvest throughout this promising land. Let us with heart and voice, word and deed, reassure our brethren in the field and give the word of cheer to our armies. I call this meeting one of reaffirmation. We are to day to reaffirm what we resolved upon fifteen months ago. What we planted in stormy spring is to be taken care of during this generous summer. What we did then was the result of instinct; now it has become a deep-rooted conviction. It was passion which then guided us; now it is principle. It may be that on the occasion of our former meeting our huzzas were louder; but now I can see it in your faces, our resolutions are deeper, and when we now strike we shall strike as doth the lightning—once and for all. We to-day reaffirm our resolution to preserve the integrity of our land, our power, our interests, and our continent. In our uttered determinations then we were wiser than we knew of. We merely said it then; we understand it now. This continent must and shall remain united, one and inseparable, and must be so until the end of time. [Applause.] This is a struggle between a rebellious confederacy and our Government; and what for? Not for the vague abstraction it purports to be, but for a remote but still more important issue—the domination of this continent. They or we will have to rule this vast land from the St. Croix to the Rio Grande, and from the Atlantic to the Pacific. And I say unto you, men of the city of New-York, shall it be we, the men of the Christian North, or shall it be sons of the sunny South, as they delight to call themselves, who are, and have proved themselves, robbers by land, and if they had a fleet upon the sea, would also be pirates. [Applause.] This is the issue, and it must be determined sooner or later. Citizens of New-York, are you men enough to say you will take the issue on your own shoulders, or leave it for your posterity? Can you look upon your babes now resting in their cradles, and bequeath to them the settlement of this great question? Will you leave it for the next generation to settle this question? [Loud cries of "No, no."] It must be determined now or never. It can be more easily settled now than by any conjunction in the future. We contend for the supremacy of our Government, and we will do so if we have to make a Thermopylæ of it, and defend the gate till all have fallen; or else we shall have to submit to a military despotism which would march over the bleeding corpses of our comrades to rule us with a rod of iron. I stand here to defend the glorious republican idea which has gained to us the laurels that crown the brow of our glorious goddess Liberty. We must defend the old republic, for if we fail the republicans of the Old World will lose heart forever. We must vindicate our republican existence, and not only vindicate it in its geographical integrity, but in its political glory—not only for ourselves, but for all mankind. ["Bravo," and applause.] The American people have learned something during the past fifteen months. I have been in the country among the farm-houses where families are more scattered, and where one taken from the originally compact family circle is missed, not only by those who form that circle, but by their neighbors. The war in those cases has been brought home to the hearts of many. I have seen women stand at the doors of their houses eagerly and anxiously waiting for the return of their wounded husbands, brothers, sons, or still more anxiously trying to learn some tidings of one who fell at Fair Oaks, Gaines' Mills, at White Oak Swamp, or elsewhere. Men die in the great city, and they are scarcely missed, except in their more immediate circle; but in the country the case is far different. These are matters of deep thought, and the people are thinking deeper than ever. They are thinking very fast. The new call is also a matter of thought, and although I cannot doubt that the quota of New-York will be filled, and quickly, too, I cannot shut my eyes to the fact that it is not responded to with that marked alacrity as that which characterized the former call. There must be a reason for this, and the Government should know it. It is not the fear of the adversary they have to encounter; but it is the fear that the Administration will not themselves carry the war through in a proper manner. The men of America have pluck, and do not fear to die for their country. They will enlist, but there is a condition which they demand. That condition is, [with great energy,] fight, fight, fight. We have had play long enough, and now must have fight. Fight and with the right hand and not with the left, and only the little finger of that hand at the best. We must have fight with the right hand. [A voice, "With both hands."] Wait till I get through. Yes, [clenching both fists and stretching them out with convulsive energy,] fight ; fight with both hands. And that is not all. I say let all the colors fight. All. From the one extreme of the Caucasian white to the other extreme of the Caucasian black—let them all fight, and let all the people that make up the different and beautiful shades between these extremes fight. Let all the people fight. Elijah saw in the heavens the chariots of fire of the Lord of Hosts. Then let the rebels have their five hundred thousand men ; we have the chariots and horses of fire, and they are round about us. We have the spirits of those heroes of old who have gone to their rest. We have also the spirits of those sages and heroes who have stood up for us in foreign lands, or who have pined in foreign dungeons for contending for our rights. And all good angels are looking down upon us. And these will guide us on to victory. I say unto you, men of New-York, we must win, and, in the end, despite all seeming adversities, the right must triumph. [Enthusiastic cheering.]

OFFICERS.

STAND No. 4.

Under charge of Committee of Arrangements,

JAMES W. WHITE, ROBERT H. McCURDY.

President.

FRANCIS LIEBER.

Vice-Presidents.

WILLIAM CURTIS NOYES,
STEWART BROWN,
MORRIS KETCHUM,
C. V. S. ROOSEVELT,
WILLIAM E. DODGE,
CYRUS W. FIELD,
WILLIAM M. EVARTS,
HENRY E. PIERREPONT,
GEORGE GRISWOLD, Jr.,
WM. H. ASPINWALL,
GULIAN C. VERPLANCK,
PETER LORILLARD,
JAMES BENKARD,
FRANCIS VINTON,
FRANCIS HALL,
JACOB A. WESTERVELT,
HERMAN RASTER,
THOMAS W. CLERKE,
JAMES B. NICHOLSON,
MARSHALL O. ROBERTS,
WOLCOTT GIBBS,
EDGAR KETCHUM,
ROBERT L. STUART,
ALEXANDER H. STEVENS,
ELIJAH FISHER,
FREDERICK KAPP,
BENJ. WELCH, Jr.,
JAMES W. FARR,
CHARLES B. SPICER,
DON ALONZO CUSHMAN,
HENRY F. SPALDING,
SIMEON BALDWIN,
GEORGE L. SCHUYLER,
RICHARD HECKSCHER,
JAMES KEARNEY WARREN,
WILLIAM ASTOR,

J. N. A. GRISWOLD,
PIERRE V. DUFLON,
ALPHEUS FOBES,
DAVID R. JAQUES,
JOHN EWEN,
EDWARD H. LUDLOW,
ROBERT LEROY,
ELLIOT C. COWDIN,
ADAM W. SPIES,
GEORGE F. WOODWARD,
SAMUEL S. SANDS,
GEORGE A. ROBBINS,
FRANCIS G. SHAW,
ROBERT G. REMSEN,
STEPHEN H. TYNG,
VALENTINE MOTT,
HENRY D. SEDGWICK,
DAVID COLDEN MURRAY,
MOSES S. BEACH,
GEORGE FOLSOM,
CAMBRIDGE LIVINGSTON,
JOHN L. ASPINWALL,
ROBERT EMMET,
JOHN D. JONES,
C. S. FRANKLIN,
HENRY FORD,
J. C. PETERS,
BENJAMIN FLOYD,
CHARLES POMROY,
JOHN MEEKS,
PARKE GODWIN,
JOHN B. WICKERSHAM,
JOHN STEVENSON,
I. M. SINGER,
CHARLES B. CLINCH,
JOSEPH FOULKE,

Clarkson N. Potter,
Joseph Bridgham,
Henry B. Smith,
Isaac Ferris,
A. E. Silliman,
Maunsell B. Field,
David Dows,
Isaac Bell,
George S. Coe,
C. L. Monell,
Henry K. Bogert,
Henry C. Murphy,
William Hegeman,

Richard Storrs Willis,
Hamilton Bruce,
Henry Kerr,
Edward Carney,
Isaac H. Bailey,
Augustus Weissman,
H. B. Stanton,
Stephen Philbin,
John R. Lawrence,
Richard M. Hoe,
Warren Ward,
Christopher Williams.

Secretaries.

Robert B. Minturn, Jr.,
Charles E. Strong,
Richard A. McCurdy,
Richard L. Suydam,
George Bruce, Jr.,
David Bishop,
W. H. L. Barnes,
A. M. Palmer,
William Bond,
Nathaniel Coles,
John H. Almy,
Cephas Brainard,
Pierre Humbert,

Samuel Williams,
Maturin Delafield,
Benjamin W. Strong,
Theodore Bronson,
William B Crocker,
Edward C. Morris,
Henry S. Fearing,
David Lydig,
Byam K. Stevens, Jr.,
James Lenox Kennedy,
A. C. Kingsland, Jr.,
George B. Satterlee,
George Griswold Haven.

PROGRAMME OF PROCEEDINGS.

STAND NO. 4.

SALUTES OF ARTILLERY by the "ANTHON LIGHT BATTERY," and by the WORKMEN employed by HENRY BREWSTER & Co.

1. GRAND MARCH, by Grafula's Grand Band.
2. JAMES W. WHITE will call the meeting to order, read the Call of the Meeting, and conduct to the Chair, FRANCIS LIEBER.
3. ROBERT H. McCURDY will read the list of Vice-Presidents and Secretaries.
4. The Chairman, FRANCIS LIEBER, will address the meeting.
5. WILLIAM CURTIS NOYES will read the ADDRESS adopted by the Convention of Committees.
6. MORRIS KETCHUM will read the RESOLUTIONS adopted by the Convention of Committees.
7. MUSIC.
8. L. E. CHITTENDEN will address the meeting.
9. MUSIC.
10. WILLIAM ALLEN BUTLER will address the meeting.
11. MUSIC.
12. W. J. A. FULLER.
13. MUSIC.
14. R. A. WITTHAUS.

The meeting was called to order by Judge JAMES W. WHITE, who read the call for the meeting, and nominated for Chairman Dr. FRANCIS LIEBER, who was elected with applause.

R. H. McCURDY read the list of Vice-Presidents and Secretaries, which was adopted.

DR. LIEBER'S REMARKS.

FELLOW-CITIZENS,—You have conferred on me the honor of presiding here on this important day. This is a war meeting. In the midst of a vast contest, in which many thousands of our brethren have already been slain, in which almost boundless treasures have been sacrificed, and in which reverses have not failed to break in upon the list of our victories, the President, first called upon by the governors of loyal States, has in turn, called upon us to furnish new bands of fellow-citizens, to send more brothers, more sons, so that this odious and shameless insurrection may at length be quelled. Resolutions will be read to you for your acceptance, expressing our undiminished loyalty, our firm adhesion to the principles for which we have already struggled so long, and which in this enormous war we prize with patriotic fervor, as the highest civil virtues in trying periods—fortitude, perseverance and tenacity to the last.

And why all this? Why this call upon the people of our city to take a renewed oath on the altar of our country, that we will be faithful and true to her, and see this war triumphantly ended, and as thoroughly carried on, until it be ended, as the ample means of a great nation will admit of.

Fellow-citizens, near the beginning of this century, there was a patriotic German youth and noble poet, who sang and fought for the independence of his country, and ultimately sealed with his death on the field what he had nobly sung. It happened that he found a sealing-ring, on which was engraved an arrow, with the motto, THROUGH. This simple arrow, and that brief word, inspired the youthful patriot with a poem, which he inscribed THROUGH, calling on his country not to waver, but to rally round the standard of his country's independence, and to fight *through* to a successful end what had so nobly been begun. Is this not a befitting motto for us to adopt in this grave time of our war? Perhaps all of us have near friends or children or brothers that have fought—many that have bled in that long Week's Battle; and ought not our war-cry to be *Through*? Ought not our policy to be *Through, through, through?* [Great applause.] Let us call to our sceptered servants, Through, and through at once! Let us call to our girded servants, Through! Let us call, when foreigners may show a desire to interfere with our own affairs, already sufficiently distressing—Hands off; we will not listen to any one until we are through! [Applause.] We ought to make it the watchword among ourselves, and call on one another, Through! We ought to call on all the young, fit to bear arms, Through, through!!

Why? Because the most sacred and dearest interests of man in his career on this earth are involved in this struggle—our material prosperity, our moral welfare, our honor, our national existence. He that shapes the history of men wills us to be a nation, and modern civilization requires *countries*. God has given us a noble country, may be the noblest on earth, which we will not, and cannot, allow ourselves to be robbed of.

We will not prove false to our trust. Shall we allow ignorance and arrogance and barbarism to cut up the great map of our heaven-united land into miserable clippings, leaving nothing but a litter of worthless pieces? [No, no! never!] Our country, our proud country, from sea to sea, with her majestic rivers, or rather, with her unique river system, and the glorious help of the canals, with her teeming mountains, and her fertile fields—our country, with all her food and fuel and substance for shelter and clothing—our country, my friends, is the primary condition of our social and political existence, and, indeed, of our own American liberty. With all due regard for our peculiar system of States, the State lines are, after all, but pencil marks on the great map. They have been changed, and will be changed again. They are not those deep grooves that history furrows, as she deeply cuts the border lines of nationalities. Not so with our country. The lines that mark her must never be changed— at least, never contracted. [Applause.]

Why? Because a country that allows foreign governments to interfere with her domestic and national affairs—that permits foreign jealousy to dictate in her councils—is disgraced and ruined; is a cripple among the nations—a vassal and not a freeman. Germany can furnish you with some warning commentaries, ever since the times of Louis the Fourteenth. Even a crowned head of Germany, a noble prince of a petty principality, told his countrymen, recently, that in modern times genuine patriotism, void of narrow provincialism, cannot prosper in a confined petty State, still less in a mere city-State. And is there no danger of foreign interference? There is; even were it only for these two reasons, that England and France suffer greatly from our civil war, and because those two powers, which have always been unfriendly to the formation of a new united power, with the only exception of Italy in our own times, do not relish the growth of United American power. It has been openly acknowledged.

Why? Because we are already in the midst of a gigantic war, exclusively waged, on our part, for a great and noble idea. Such wars cannot be stopped at will; as little as the tide can be bid to retire by a mop, as little as the Reformation could be calmed and stopped by the agreement of some ecclesiastics. Can we adopt peace founded upon the rending of this country? Where will you rend it? how will you keep peace? Do you believe that we would have peace for a single twelve-month after a division, the mere thought of which makes us shudder? We speak the same language, inhabit one undivided country, have the same literature, the same form of thoughts, the same mould of feelings, the same institutions, except that one deplorable one; we would daily and hourly influence one another, and what with their unpunished pride and selfishness, their maddened and confused ambition, and their enthronement of gigantic error, we would not have rest, except by a total and unpardonable submission to them, and not even then. There is a law that pervades all history, because it pervades each house, that in the same degree as nature has destined people to live in the bonds of affection and good-will, so will their quarrels be bitter, and their mutual irritation be grievous, when they once separate in acrimony and hostility. Brothers quarrel bitterest, when they quarrel at all. We had better fight it out. Complete victory alone can lead to a reconcilement, and revised views and amended feelings; and therefore I say, Through, through! [Great applause.]

When I say that we ought to shout this same *through*, in the loudest accents to our people fit to enlist, I must not be understood to have harbored any fear that there is not a sufficient degree of patriotism in the breasts of our people. Far from it. Never has a people shown itself more patriotic, more patient and forbearing, more ready.

It happens that this very morning I received a letter from a distinguished lawyer and legislator—a true Union man—in St. Louis, Missouri, and in that letter there is a passing passage which, (if you will permit me to read it,) you will perceive chimes in with the theme which occupies our attention now. He says:

"That among those best informed no apprehension is felt for the new call for volunteers. Governor Gamble has received more than fifty letters, some before, some since the call, from men in all parts of this State, (Missouri,) asking authority to recruit companies, regiments, and in one case, a brigade—the last from an officer just recovered from a wound, who is confident of raising it. In Illinois I hear of the same spirit; the only thing which may for a while check rapid enlistments, being the abundant harvest now being gathered." [Cheers.]

So far my Missouri friend. But there is another thing that may temporarily interfere, or at least somewhat retard the desired enlistment. The call for recruits is comparatively a small one. The President, you know, calls for three hundred thousand men. This is, in fact, a large number of men, but, comparatively speaking, considering the population of the North, it is a small number. Only about fifty thousand are required from this State. Now who doubts if there had been a necessity for the President to call for the services of every one who can shoulder a musket, that the people would rush *en masse*, in response to the call? But when a limited number is required and called for, many of the fifty thousand who are wanted, are disposed to say, "I need not volunteer; my services will not be required, for my neighbor will go." For that reason I am inclined to believe that we ought to resort to the drafting law. I know that does not sound well to the ears of the Americans, because drafting has been made use of by despotic governments, and has been resorted to in the South, by what I have not the least doubt is a despotic government. But drafting is not necessarily a despotic measure. The advantage of it would be, that it would make recruiting and enlisting more regular. If the Government should adopt such a measure, I think it would work well. Drafting, too, would touch the wealthy idlers, at least so far as to make them contribute a round sum for a substitute, if they should insist upon thrusting away the sword which their country offers them, and decline the honor to fight for their imperiled country. At any rate, as men are wanted speedily, the adoption of this system would give us the men immediately, while the small number called for, and the approaching harvest, may have a tendency to prevent the rush of young men which would otherwise take place.

Fellow-citizens, I have spoken a longer time than is appropriate for the initiatory remarks of a presiding officer; but who can help it, in times like these, on themes like ours?

The declaration and resolutions will now be read to you.

Dr. LIEBER sat down amid prolonged applause.

The ADDRESS was then read by W. J. A. FULLER, and the RESOLUTIONS by FRANCIS KETCHUM, and they were adopted with unanimity and cheers.

SPEECH OF L. E. CHITTENDEN.

FELLOW-CITIZENS,—I have taken myself out of the changeless routine of the Treasury Department, in Washington, and have come here hoping to find myself among a live people. [A voice, "You will."] Yes, I hope there is a people here alive to the necessities of the present moment. Fellow-citizens, the voice of sixteen months of war, tells us in tones that must be heeded, that the time for talking has passed; that the time has come, when it is the duty of every citizen of a loyal State, to offer his services to the Government in whatever capacity they may be most available. If I had not offered mine before I came here, I would not appear before you to-day. [Applause.] I am so full of this subject, that I do not like to trust myself to talk about it. I come from a city, and that city the capital of this nation, in which we were cut off for a week from communication with you, by traitors—where barricaded corridors, forts, and earthworks, spoke eloquently of attacks impending from an armed enemy. This was a long year ago, and yet, after all the preparation, after all the expense which that year has witnessed, it is not eight weeks since loyal men were alarmed for the safety of that very city! We who live in close proximity to the enemy, nay, with the minions of that enemy by hundreds among us, appreciate the dangers by which we are surrounded. Men of New-York, I wish for one short hour you could be made to realize the necessity which this moment presses on you. Do you consider this Government worth preserving? [Cries of Yes! Yes!] Is this free Republic, planted by your ancestors, nourished by their blood, left to you as their richest legacy, worth preserving! Do you feel, that you, your wives, your children, have an interest in it which ought to be dearer than their lives? [Loud cries of "Yes."] Yes, you do. Then let me tell you, that perhaps the day may be approaching, it may be near, when every one of you who can shoulder a musket or draw a sabre, will be obliged to do it if this nation is to live.

Gentlemen, the South went into this war with a purpose. [A voice, "That's so."] They have never debated questions about which our Congress and our Government have wasted so much time. These rebels declared at first, "We propose to overthrow your Government, to utterly destroy it." They began by confiscating every dollar of debts owed by Southern men to the North. They followed it up by imprisoning every man within their reach who was in sympathy with the Union and the Government which we inherited from Washington and the Fathers of the Republic; not only that, but they said to us in effect, "We propose to fight you, to take your property, to destroy your lives. To accomplish this, we will use every means within our grasp; we will use Indian savages as our allies; we will tear open the graves of your dead, and make merchandise of the bones from which the worms have not yet stripped the uncorrupted flesh; we will go into battle with the 'no quarter' cry of the red-handed barbarian upon our lips, and the black flag of the pirate waving over our heads." Such ideas as these fired the Southern heart sixteen months ago when they fired the first gun at Fort Sumter, and the history of the times tells how well they have carried them into practice. What have we been doing all this time ? We have been treating these gentlemen with the most distinguished consideration. [A voice, "That's so."] We could not confiscate their property! Oh, no! *Nothing but a life interest in it!* All the rest we are bound under the Constitution to protect. But, gentlemen, it is no pleasure to me, it cannot be to any one, to dwell upon the policy which we have pursued since the rebellion broke out. Out of it stands patent and undisguised, this great, this important, this, to many a household, solemn fact—that the soil of rebel States has been crimsoned with the blood of a hundred and twenty-five thousand brave and loyal men, and still rebellion is as defiant as ever. Has not this gone far enough ? [Loud cries of "Yes, yes!"] Has not the time come to declare *war*, and a vigorous war against the South ! War with all its consequences to persons and to property ? [" Yes, yes !" and tremendous cheers.] Yes, and would to Heaven the voice with which you speak it, might reach the Congress and the Cabinet which just now need encouragement like that !

At this moment a procession of sailors with bands and banners passed by. It was composed of ship-carpenters from the Navy Yard, and the enthusiasm increased when three rousing cheers were given for the Navy. The scene was a splendid one as they marched round the Square.

Mr. CHITTENDEN continued :

This is no time for fault-finding or complaint. I care not, I do not ask, who has been responsible for the policy upon which the war has been conducted. We have tried it—it has failed, and is it not high time to change it ? [Loud cries of "Yes!"] Let us have no more protection of the persons or the property of disloyal men. I have met officers of our army from the valley of the Shenandoah who drew a picture of the vigorous manner in which the property of rebels there was guarded. These men were in the Southern army—all of them. Their women derided and abused Union soldiers. Sick men lay in miserable hovels and died there, while splendid residences of rebel owners stood close by. A soldier could not take so much as a chicken without being punished for it. By and by Stonewall Jackson sweeps up the valley with an overwhelming force, and our retreating troops are shot down from the windows of the very houses they have saved from destruction. [A voice, "Destroy the inhabitants."] Gentlemen, I assert that it is time to proclaim to every Winchester in the so-called Southern Confederacy, that there shall not be left one article above ground in such a town, that fire can consume ! [Great enthusiasm.] Let our policy be every piece of property belonging to a rebel that will do a Union man good, take it ; if it won't do him any good, burn it. [Tremendous cheers and cries of " That's the talk."] Gentlemen, we have been fighting the rebels and Providence, too. That is an unequal warfare. The slavery question lies at the bottom of the whole. That was the cause of this rebellion, we all know. [Cheers, and cries of "That's so."] I believe it is one of the eternal decrees of Providence, that with this war slavery in this republic shall die. [Loud cheering.] When the

10

North accepts this truth, and goes into the war understanding it, and prepared to carry it out, then disaster and disgrace will cease to attend our arms. Then, and not till then, shall we be successful.

I have no special admiration for the negro, as all know who know me. But the negro is a great fact in this contest, and we cannot get rid of him if we would. Now, I would treat him in this connection as I would treat any other person or thing. Is he of use to the enemy? Take him away! Can he be made use of to our men? Let them use him! Why all this idle sensitiveness on account of the negro? He can dig a ditch; he can build an earthwork; he can do a thousand things which wear out the lives of your soldiers, better than they. Let him do them! My doctrine is to put this whole subject under the control of the commanders of our armies. They understand it better than you or I. Do not hamper them with restrictions or conditions. Only let this fact be thundered into the ears of every disloyal man North or South. There is no law, there is no officer, civil or military, which will aid a rebel to recapture his slave. [Cries of good, and cheers.] The armies of the Union are not slave hunters, [Cheers,] and the slave of a rebel master who has performed one act in the service of the Government, and in putting down this rebellion, is from that moment a free man, and the strong arm of the nation shall crush the traitor who seeks again to enslave him. [Cheers.]

We are told now that another element is to enter into this war. Rumors are rife of foreign intervention. [Cries of "Let them come."] So say I. It is by no grace or favor of European monarchies, and of England especially, that this nation lives. We expect England to strike us just when and where we are weakest. She would not be true to herself or her history if she did not. I do not undervalue the importance of foreign intervention. I do not know but some such event is needed to rouse the North, and make her put forth her strength. Let England and France now attack us, and the North would be electrified. That English or French regiment is not raised, nor ever will be, that can reach a point twenty miles inland in any Northern State. There is not a stone by the roadside that would not blush for itself, if it had not behind it a true man and a trusty rifle in such an event. [Loud cheering.]

Mr Chittenden complimented our generals, but insisted that there was a defect somewhere in the management of this war. We were thirty millions of people against four, and yet upon every important battlefield the forces of the rebels had outnumbered ours—in the last battles before Richmond, two to one. The North must go into the field with the same energy and numbers as the South. General Pope had announced the true theory of war. Adopt the policy his orders inaugurate. We have had too much of that style of war which is always looking for lines of defence and ways of retreat. Let us look only at what line of defence the rebels have, that we may march upon it. Let us observe their line of retreat for there lies our way. Subsist our armies on the enemy. Pay our troops from the gold of the enemy. Have done with permanent stores, with supply trains and baggage transportation. The views of such men as Pope must now control our armies; then will the war be carried on in earnest, and then will it be successful.

He concluded amid applause.

SPEECH OF WILLIAM ALLEN BUTLER.

Mr. WILLIAM ALLEN BUTLER was next introduced by the Chairman.

FELLOW-CITIZENS,—This is a meeting for business. We are not here, on a gala day, to hear ourselves talk, but to act in a great crisis. [Cheers.] We have heard, from the speaker who preceded me, what we have heard before, once and again, that the capital is in danger. The appeal now made to us by the Government is not a new one. We have responded to it before. If I am asked how we have responded, I point to the gallant Seventh, I point to the seventy-two regiments which have been organized and equipped in the Empire City since the outbreak of the rebellion. [Cheers.] I point to Wall-street and its banks. I point to every citizen of every class and country, from the private in the Sixty-ninth [loud cheers] to the men of largest wealth and influence, and I say that to every summons of duty New-York has given a prompt and a noble response. More than twelve months ago, around this very Square, at the same hour as on this day, we met for a like purpose. Not far from the spot where I am now speaking to you, a man stood up and spoke these words, "This rebellion must be put down. It may take seventy thousand men. What then? We have them. It may take seven hundred thousand men. What then? We have them." These were the words of Colonel Baker. [Cheers.]

He fell at Ball's Bluff, the victim, if not of military treason, of military incompetency. He is gone—we are here. The seventy thousand men are gone. Six hundred thousand men have been given, but the rebellion is not put down. The question for us to-day is, not whose fault is it. The simple question is, shall it be put down? [Cries of "Yes!"] We are not here to criticise or to blame, but to ask ourselves what is our individual duty. What is your duty—what is mine? What will you do? [Cries of "All we can."] What will I do? I reply, every man of us, who can go in person, should go at once. If a man cannot go himself let him get his neighbor to go. If he can neither go himself nor send his neighbor, let him give what he can in aiding others to go. Let every man give; the rich from their abundance, the poor from their toil. This is our part. We may have our views and our preferences, but this is not the time for them. This rebellion will never be subdued unless we respond as we ought to, to this new call to duty. Will you do it? ["Yes!"]

As for the Government, the policy it needs is summed up in the single word—fight. ["That's it."] I would say this to Abraham Lincoln, and to every general and every man in the field. Fight with every weapon and use every means of success. As our armies advance, every man, who is a friend, should be welcomed, whatever his condition or color. [Cheers.] If he can dig, give him a pick. If he can fight, give him a musket. Take aid wherever we can get it. I read yesterday that James Buchanan had given $100 as a contribution to the sick and wounded Pennsylvania volunteers! Even his money I would take. [Laughter and cheers.] It may help to smooth the pillow or stanch the wound of some brave fellow who has fallen in the effort to redress the wrongs his treachery inflicted. Let the Government pursue this plain policy, and let every man sustain it by all the means in his power, and with God's blessing on our arms we are as certain to succeed as to-day's sun is sure to set. [Loud applause.]

THE YOUNG MEN'S MEETING.

STAND No. 5.

This stand was under the auspices of Committees of the Mercantile Library Association, and the Young Men's Christian Association.

These bodies not being represented in the Convention of Committees, but at a late hour expressing a desire to participate in the great loyal demonstration, were invited to do so. The proceedings on this stand were conducted by the young men without interference from the General Committee of Management.

BENJ. F. MANIERRE called the meeting to order and introduced, as presiding officer, Major-General JOHN C. FREMONT, who came forward amid great applause, and called upon the Rev. JOSEPH T. DURYEA to commence the exercises with prayer.

THE PRAYER.

O God our Heavenly Father, the God of our fathers, and our God. We look up to Thee at the beginning of this meeting for Thy presence. We acknowledge Thee to be the Lord. We acknowledge Thee to be the God of the whole earth. Our nation is dependent upon Thee, and from Thee we receive our national existence. Secure us in these our times of peril, and unite all the hearts of this great people with the sentiments of purpose, and of ardor, and zeal. Concentrate all the powers and resources of this country to our salvation from the enemy which threatens our national existence. O God, fill the hearts of the young with the power of the spirit of self-sacrifice, and let not one of us withhold our gifts and our powers, and influence, or our children, from this cause, which may give to us Liberty, and benefit the race of mankind. We pray that Thou wilt bless the President of the United States, and all who have authority under him, giving them wisdom, giving them courage, singleness of purpose, and innocence of heart. May the foreign nations of the earth understand, that our single aim is to remove the enemy before us, and reunite all parts of the land under the control of one Government. We pray that thou wilt bless the army on the field, the officers who are now present, and those who in our hospitals, are on the bed of sickness. Give courage to them, and accept us all for Jesus Christ's sake, Amen!

Mr. FRANK W. BALLARD read the list of Vice-Presidents, as follows:—

Vice-Presidents.

Hon. BENJ F. MANIERRE,
FREDERICK C. WAGNER,
SAMUEL W. STEBBINS,
A. D. F. RANDOLPH,
FRANK W. BALLARD,
ERASMUS STERLING,
A. J. H. DUGANNE,
GEORGE T. HOPE,
E. DELAFIELD SMITH,
VINCENT COLYER,
STEWART L. WOODFORD,
CEPHAS BRAINERD,
CHARLES OSGOOD,
JOHN CRERAR,
GEORGE C. WOOD,
WM. H. WICKHAM,
JAMES WHITE,
CHARLES F. ALLEN,
HARVEY H. WOODS,
WILLIAM A. MARTEN,
Rev. A. H. BURLINGHAM,
HENRY J. ARMSTRONG,
WILLARD HARVEY,
JOHN K. MYERS,
HENRY B. HYDE,
PHILIP FRANKENHEIMER,
TREADWELL KETCHUM,
RICHARD S. STORRS,
Capt. CHARLES C. NOTT,
JOHN M. LETTS,
CHARLES S. MESSINGER,
Rev. JOSEPH T. DURYEA,
THADDEUS B. WAKEMAN,
J. EVARTS TRACY,
AUSTIN LEAKE,
MARK HOYT,

E. C. JOHNSON,
DEXTER A. HAWKINS,
GEORGE H. MATHEWS,
CHARLES T. RODGERS,
WILLIAM M. FRANKLIN,
Col. JAMES FAIRMAN,
JAMES W. NEWTON,
CALEB B. KNEVALS,
Rev. CHAUNCEY MURRAY,
GEORGE W. CLARKE,
JAMES C. HOLDEN,
STEPHEN H. TYNG, Jr.,
Capt. CHARLES A. MOORE,
JOSEPH W. LESTER,
HENRY BEENY,
Col. JAMES McKAYE,
EDWARD COLGATE,
LEONARD D. WHITE,
FREDERICK OLMSTEAD,
Rev. H. B. RIDGWAY,
Col. JAMES W. SAVAGE,
EPES E. ELLERY,
HENRY WILSON,
Rev. T. RALSTON SMITH,
AUSTIN ABBOTT,
Lieut. THOMAS L. THORNELL,
Capt. A. V. MEEKS,
D. WILLIS JAMES,
W. B. ROBERTS,
ROBERT COLBY,
SAMUEL S. CONSTANT,
CHARLES A. STETSON, Jr.,
ALEX. PROUDFOOT,
D. H. GILDERSLEEVE,
WILLIAM HAGUE,

Mr. HOWARD then read the following list of Secretaries —

Secretaries.

S. HASTINGS GRANT,
D. S. RIDDLE,
CHARLES NORDHOFF,
JAMES L. HASTIE,
WM. W. HAGUE,
Lieut. B. T. MARTEN,
A. K. MACMILLAN,
R. M. STREBEIGH,
RICHARD VALLANT,
ROBT. McBURNEY,
FREDERICK W. DOWNER,
W. S. MATHEWS,
DAVID DRAKE,
VERANUS MORSE, M. D.,
CHARLES H. SWORDS,
DANL. W. BERDAN,
THADDEUS V. TABER,

CHARLES NETTLETON,
EDWARD P. MORRIS,
JAMES WARD SMYTHE,
E. P. TIBBALS,
JAMES S. STEARNS,
EDWARD A. MANN,
CHARLES E. WILBUR,
J. HOWARD,
JNO. HENRY HALL,
OETER M. MYERS,
O. V. COFFIN,
WILLIAM D. JONES,
MANTON MARBLE,
HIRAM CALKINS,
FRANCIS A. HALL,
T. G. SHEARMAN,
JAMES McGEE.

GEN. FREMONT'S SPEECH.

Gen. FREMONT then rose, amid deafening applause. He said:—

It is hardly necessary to say that this great assemblage has been called to consider the situation of the country, with the object of adopting such measures as will enable you to respond most immediately and most effectively to the President's call for troops. But at the same time it is expected that this occasion will be used for such an expression of your feelings and opinions as will satisfy the country, that the enthusiasm which characterized your meeting held here last year, as now, has become a settled resolve, and that it is not in the ideas or possibilities of the day that you should consent to a dismemberment of your national territory. [Loud cheers, and cries of "Never."] The people have realized that a decisive struggle, which would tax their utmost energies, is now to come, and that upon the issue of this struggle depends the life of the nation. [Immense applause.] The South has resolved itself into a great army, to the support of which all its industrial energies and resources are directed. You, too, will find it necessary to call into immediate activity your immense resources to meet the emergency. [Cheers.] For a brief time now war must be the business of the nation. [Cheers.] You must show your soldiers that they have not only your admiration and gratitude for the services they have rendered to you, but that they can rely upon your cordial and prompt support, and that they, too, have their great reserves in the masses of the people. [Cheers.] By this expression the Executive will feel assured of an intelligent, harmonious and effective co-operation, and foreign Governments will recognize that we intend to maintain our historic place in the family of nations, at the head of the great democratic idea, [cheers,] and that for the sake of liberty we are resolved to maintain this Union. [Loud cheers.] The men chosen to address you to-day, are among those in whom you are accustomed to place confidence, and whose opinions on these subjects more or less reflect your own. [Immense applause.] I will now introduce to you other speakers.

Dr. RUFUS W. CLARK was then introduced.

SPEECH OF REV. RUFUS W. CLARK, D. D.

MR. PRESIDENT AND FELLOW-CITIZENS,—I shall take my text on this occasion from one of the books of Daniel—not Daniel the prophet, but Daniel Webster. [Laughter.] For he has somewhere said or written this noble sentiment, ' Liberty and Union, one and inseparable, now and forever." [Cheers.] The Union is represented by the vast concourse gathered around me, embracing men of all political parties and creeds. Liberty is represented in the person of General Fremont, who presides on this occasion. [Tremendous cheers.] And the pledge that they shall be one and inseparable floats over our heads in the star-spangled banner.

I remember that very early in the struggle, somewhere down South, they had a funeral, and they took the old flag, and with mock solemnity, buried it ; and they supposed that was the last of the American flag. But, gentlemen, I believe in the doctrine of the resurrection, [applause] ; and I believe that the sacred emblem of our national rights and honor, even from that soil, cursed with rebellion to-day, will rise again and proudly float over that and every other defiant State, and represent in the future—as it has in the past—a united, prosperous and happy people.

The incident reminds me of an ignorant politician, who was sent by his neighbors to an adjoining county to ascertain what a tax was for, that had been levied. He was told that it was to promote the navy and prevent an insurrection. On returning home he was asked if he had ascertained what the tax was for. "Oh, yes," said he, "it is to *promote knavery and prevent the resurrection.*" [Great laughter.] I have no doubt but that the taxes at the South will promote knavery, but they will not prevent the resurrection of that flag around which we rally to-day, and to the maintenance of which we renewedly consecrate our lives, our fortunes, and our sacred honor. [Cheers.]

But, fellow-citizens, the hour is solemn. We meet at a momentous crisis in our national history. The republic is in danger. This colossal and iniquitous rebellion must be met; it must be grappled with and crushed now. I am not here to appeal to your passions. I do not stand before this mighty gathering of American citizens simply to make a speech. I am here to kindle anew the fire of your patriotism : to awaken, if possible, an increased energy and devotion to the cause so dear to our hearts ; the cause that embraces the interests of civilization, human liberty, and the progress of society in the arts, education, and religion. I am here to urge you to rally to the call of our noble President, and to join the hosts already in the field, who are doing their utmost to roll back the tide of rebellion, and preserve the precious institutions bequeathed to us by our fathers. [Applause.]

In this struggle, we aim, first, at the security of our national existence. We desire to live among the nations of the earth, and God helping us, we will maintain the Republic against all the opposition, domestic or foreign, that may be brought to bear against us. [Immense applause.] Not a few persons in Europe, especially in England, have blamed us for this. We have been censured for desiring to exist, and for not quietly acquiescing in the dismemberment of our nation. The people of England have declared that our republican institutions were a failure. [A voice in the crowd, "They lie."] Yes, those who say it do lie ; and they will have to lie quietly until we can attend to their sneers and threats. I had supposed, until recently, that England was distinguished for her civilization, her intense humanity, and devotion to the doctrine of human rights. I had supposed that her statesmen and leaders of public opinion were in favor of cultivating peaceful relations with the other powers of the earth ; and, surely, we have done nothing to provoke her enmity. Rather, we have done all in our power to maintain a cordial and generous friendship. We have bestowed upon her authors and eminent men, who have visited our shores, every mark of attention. Some years ago, when her Irish citizens were starving, we ladened our ships of war with provisions for their relief, and gladly gave of our abundance to the needy. When a lost British ship, in the Arctic regions, was found by an American captain, she was brought to one of our ports, carefully and thoroughly refitted, and returned to the Queen as an expression of our good-will and respect for her administration. And how recently these streets were thronged by our enthusiastic citizens, to do honor to the young Prince of Wales, the representative of the British throne. No demonstration could have been more marked or sincere ; none could have sprung from purer feelings, a loftier sentiment than that which greeted the son of the Queen. And now, in the hour of our embarrassment and peril, what return do we receive from that people ? Where are their sympathies, as expressed through their public press ? Should the child of royalty again visit us and pass through our streets, I apprehend that we should allow him to go on his way in silence, and no more waste our attentions upon a government incapable of appreciating an act of pure and generous national friendship. And we shall ask neither of England or of any other nation on the globe, the privilege of existing : and when the pernicious traitors at home are annihilated, I believe that we shall have leisure and ability to see that we are not interfered with by the nations of Europe. [Immense cheers.]

Fellow-citizens, we are here also to maintain our Government. What is Government? It is the sentiments of the whole community embodied in laws, which certain officers are selected to execute. The Government is created to protect property, regulate the intercourse and relations of citizens, and defend human life. Without a Government, there can be no such thing as property- that is, the right of possession. In a savage state, no man can hold land, houses or merchandise, for there is no centralized authority to enforce his claims, or protect his rights. And the man who rebels against a just, good Government, does all in his power to weaken your hold upon your property, and reduce society to a condition of barbarism. He dethrones order and law, and inaugurates insecurity and anarchy.

Government also exists to protect human liberty and life. The man, therefore, who strikes a blow at the Government, labors to destroy that protection. He is the foe of society. Rebellion is national suicide, and no punishment can be too great for those who have plotted the destruction of such a Government as ours, and who seek the destruction of a Republic that has given happiness and prosperity to so many millions of freemen. [Cheers.]

Gentlemen, we are here also to preserve and perpetuate the American Union. Now this Union was not created by a compact of the States. The idea of State sovereignty is a delusion. Before we achieved our independence, which was the beginning of our national life, the colonies derived all their powers from the British crown. They were under that crown until the moment that they passed under the authority of the Federal Government. They did not cede their authority to the Federal Government, for they had none to cede. Independence was declared and achieved by the people of the whole country, and not by individual States. The United States Constitution was framed and adopted by the people, and the right of secession is nowhere recognized. It is neither tolerated in the instrument itself, nor in the terms upon which the Constitution was adopted and ratified by the people of the several States. The authorities on this point are clear and incontrovertible. We are struggling also to maintain the principle of human liberty.

Do you ask where do we get that principle? I reply, not from the Declaration of American Independence, but from the human soul, where the Almighty planted it. That declaration simply expressed what has ever existed in the breast of man ; and if you will consult the writings of Hamilton, Jefferson, Jay, Washington, and other of the early American heroes, you will find that the great struggle then was, not simply for the freedom of this nation, but *for the great doctrine of human rights*. They fought for the liberty of man, endowed by his Creator with certain inalienable rights. We also fight to-day for liberty, and in proportion as we smite the cause of the Rebellion, as well as the Rebellion itself, the Almighty will help us, and crown our arms with victory. [Great applause.]

And I deem it very appropriate, that the noble General who is with us to-day, who first placed the American flag upon the summit of the Rocky Mountains, and who gave freedom to California, should be the first to sound the bugle notes of emancipation at the head of the army. [Immense cheering.] And although the Government did not at that time sustain him, still those bugle notes have, ever since, been rolling over the plains, and reverberating through the hills and valleys, all over the country. And when those notes are gathered up and set to music, and our armies march to that music, then will they move on to honor and to victory. Let us then, one and all, respond to the call of our President, and let us inscribe in letters of gold upon our banners, the sentiment with which I began, " Liberty and Union, one and inseparable, now and forever." [Prolonged cheers.]

SPEECH OF HON. E. DELAFIELD SMITH.

General FREMONT, the chairman, then introduced the Hon. E. DELAFIELD SMITH, the United States District Attorney, who was received with great enthusiasm, and spoke as follows :—

MEN OF NEW-YORK,—This is, in truth, a colossal demonstration. The eye can hardly reach the boundaries of these compact thousands. It would be in vain for the voice to attempt it. The people have come in their might. They have come in their majesty. They have "come as the winds come when forests are rended." They have "come as the waves come when navies are stranded." We are here to-day, not to speak and acclaim, but to act and incite to action. [Applause.] We know that this monster rebellion cannot be spoken down; it must be fought down! [Cheers.]

We are assembled to animate each other to renewed efforts and nobler sacrifices in behalf of our imperiled country. There is hardly one of us who has not, at this hour, some endeared relative on the bloody fields of Virginia. The voices of our armed and suffering brethren literally cry to us from the ground. To-day we hear them. To-day let us heed them. [Applause.] The call for fresh troops comes to us from a loved and trusted President—from faithful and heroic Generals. [Loud cheers.] This day determines that it shall be answered. [Renewed cheers.] Let each act as though specially commissioned to obtain recruits for a sacred service. [Applause.]

Fremont is here. You have heard his voice. He has told us to uphold our Government and sustain our Generals in the field. Whatever officer may go to battle with the President's commission, will be made strong by a loyal people's prayers and confidence. [Loud cheering.]

The army and navy, the President, the Cabinet and the Congress, have done all that can now be effected by them. The issue to-day is with the people. Do you ask activity on the part of the President? Recall his personal labor and supervision in the council and the field. Do you seek a policy? Look to his solemn conference with the loyalists of the border States. [Cheers.] Do you demand legislation? Witness the matured laws that Congress has spread upon the statute-book. A jurist from the bench of our highest tribunal once declared a maxim which shocked the country and the world. It is ours, with our representatives, to respond: A REBEL "HAS NO RIGHTS WHICH A WHITE MAN IS BOUND TO RESPECT!" [Loud and long continued cheering, with waving of hats and handkerchiefs.]

A traitor cannot own a loyalist of any race. Nor can "service be due" to national conspirators, except at the call of public justice. [Laughter and applause.]

The limits of civilized warfare must and will be observed; but those limits are broad as the boundaries of the ocean, and they lie far beyond the lives and the treasure of traitors in arms. [Cheers.] In this mortal combat between the enemies and the friends of republican liberty, wherein treason scruples at nothing, patriots must neglect no means that God and nature have placed in their hands. [Loud cheers.] These institutions were reared on the ruins of British pride. Their foundations must be reconstructed on the crumbled pretensions of southern oligarchs. [Renewed cheers.] We must, and we will, repel force by force. They who press an iron heel upon the heart of our noble nation, must perish by the sword of her avenging sons. God grant the time may be near when every rebel leader may say his prayers, and bite the dust, or hang as high as Haman. If we are wise, and true, and brave, the American Union, like the sun in the heavens, shall be clouded but for a night. Still shall it move onward, and every obstacle in its pathway be withered and crushed. [Renewed and continued cheering.]

Victory, indeed, cannot be won except by arms. Our institutions were the gift of the wounded and dead of the armies of Washington. Shakspeare said, and we re-utter in a higher sense,

"Things bought with blood must be by blood maintained."

Look to our armies and rally the people to swell their wasted ranks. Go, you who can. And spare neither men nor money to enable others to march to battle. [Cheers.]

Let loyal men permit no question to distract or divide them. Care not what a man's theories may be, so that his heart feels and his hand works for the Union. Every citizen, North or South, who prays for the success of our arms, and who labors for the vindication of our Constitution, whatever may be his politics or opinions, is a patriot. [Cheers.] They who condemn any class of our fellow-citizens because of differences on collateral issues—those who declare that a loyal abolitionist is on a level with an armed secessionist—are wrong in head, or at heart unsound. [Applause.]

Let assertions like this be at an end. Let all loyal men and all loyal journals abandon arguments which bear the dull and counterfeit ring of traitor philosophy. [Loud applause.]

For the rest—for those who not alone *seem*, but *are*, disloyal—let the people arise in their might, and silence them all, whether they speak in the street to the few, or seek, through the public press, to poison the many. Law, in many things, cannot go so far, nor accomplish so much, as determined public opinion. [Cheers.] While men like Andrew Johnson, of Tennessee, with herculean strength, strike, in their districts, at the hydra of rebellion, shall not we, in New-York, war upon the spirit of secession in every form? [Applause, and cries of " We will."] The old flag must be the paramount object of all. It will be loved by the faithful. By the false, it must be feared. [Vociferous cheering.]

They talk of a distinction between fidelity to the Government and devotion to the Administration. In the day of national danger or disaster, the two sentiments are inseparable. Distrust him who professes the one only to disclaim the other. [Applause.] When the tempest howls, no prayer breathed for the ship forgets the pilot at her helm. [Applause and cheers.]

Loyalty knows no conditions. Stand by the Government! Scrutinize its action; but do it like earnest patriots—not like covert traitors. Stand by the Administration! In times like these, party spirit should be lulled. That spirit was hushed in the era of the Revolution—in the days of Madison and Monroe—and when the hero of New Orleans crushed the rising form of nullification. Our fathers stood by Jackson as their sires sustained Washington. It is our privilege to uphold the arm of a President, great and pure, who will share their glory on the page of history. [Loud cheering.]

I must trespass no longer. [Cries of " Go on, go on."] No, fellow-citizens; I will bid you farewell. Our illustrious Secretary of State has this day given to the army the only son not already in the public service. Let us emulate his spirit of sacrifice, and think nothing too dear to offer on the altar of our country.

Mr. SMITH spoke with a clear, loud voice, and retired in the midst of most enthusiastic cheering.

SPEECH OF JOSEPH HOXIE, ESQ.

Mr. JOSEPH HOXIE was next introduced, was warmly received, and spoke as follows:

They say this is the young men's stand, intended more especially for the young men, and should any one say, " Why, Hoxie has the impudence to claim the honor of belonging to that patriotic part of our fellow-citizens, the young men," I should simply say, " Why, my friends, I have belonged to the Young Men's Committee for more than forty years." [Laughter and applause.] And now, before addressing you, very briefly, I propose that we all unite in singing the " Star-Spangled Banner," and I want about five acres of this audience to join in the chorus. [Great cheering.]

The " Star-Spangled Banner " was then sung by a glee club on the platform, thousands upon thousands of voices in the immense crowd joining in the chorus with a most thrilling effect.

Mr. HOXIE then resumed, as follows :—

The reverend gentlemen who preceded me took for his text those undying words of the lamented Webster, written, I am sure, in letters that are never to be erased from the heart of every true American. In the very brief remarks I have to make to you my text shall be my country. I did not expect, my fellow-citizens, ever to be called upon to address an assemblage such as this and upon such an occasion as this. Who of us ever imagined, when last we met at this place, that at this time we should be called on, as we are, by that noble patriot at the head of the Government for 300,000 freemen more to crush out this accursed rebellion; but so it is, and we have met here to-day to respond with all our hearts to that patriotic call of our Chief Magistrate. [Applause.] And all we have upon earth are ready to be sacrificed upon the altar of our country. [Cries of "Good," "good."] This Union must be preserved, and it shall be preserved. [Great cheering.] And it is not worth while for us now, my fellow-citizens, to undertake to criticise the conduct of those who may have commanded our armies in the field, and of those who have directed the legislation in the Congress of the United States, or of the chosen councillors of the President of the United States—the heads of the various departments. It is in vain for us to say that this man has done wrong; that this man should be removed or that man appointed. No, my fellow-citizens, we come here not to ask any such contemptible question as this. We have come here to ask this question: What can we do, what shall we do, in this exigency of the country, to preserve the integrity of the Union and the Constitution of the United States? [Great applause.] That is the question we are called upon to answer. If some of our generals have made a mistake, what of it? Let him, and let him only, throw stones at them who never made a mistake himself. [Cries of "Good," "good."] No, gentlemen, we all confide in the patriotism, the integrity, the honesty of that glorious statesman at the head of the Government—[great applause]—confide in those whom he has chosen to enable him to carry on the Government. Don't say, as I have heard a gentleman say within the last forty-eight hours, that these 300,000 men will never be raised until Stanton is removed. Voices, " They will."] We do not come here to respond to any such sentiments as that. We come here to tender all we have to the President of the United States and to those associated with him in administering the affairs of this Government. Never before in my life—a somewhat advanced one—have I felt the weight of the responsibility that should attach to every good citizen as I feel it to-day. But I am not alone in this, as these thousands and tens of thousands before me bear willing witness. The time for talking, as was well said by my predecessor, has passed; the time for decisive action has arrived. Now, what can we—what shall we do—what ought we to do to save our bleeding country? [Voices, "Fight."] Our glorious flag was stained with the blood of my father, and oh how unworthy I should be of every throb of blood that courses in my veins, if I were not willing to sacrifice everything I have upon the earth sooner than to see it trail in the dust. [Great cheering.] Hear you not, my friends, wafted upon every Southern breeze, the groans of the wounded and the dying from the field of battle—of our brothers, our sons and our friends? Shall they cry to you in vain? [Loud cries of "No, no."] Hear you not the wails of the widow and the orphan, demanding of you and me that if we cannot restore to them their loved and their lost ones, that we shall swear this day to avenge their fate. We have come here to pledge ourselves before God and our country that so long as we have an arm to raise or a voice to speak they shall both be used in defence of this glorious Union. [Great applause.] What would you think, fellow-citizens, if, when a fire was devouring your residence, the fireman of an engine company, instead of putting on the hose to the engine and playing away upon the fire, should sit down and begin to criticise the conduct of those who constructed the building, or those who perhaps set it on fire, and while they were settling the question of who was to blame the building should be utterly given to the flames and destroyed What would you think of a fire company that would do that? But what would you think, when the flames are wrapping in destruction the nation's house, this temple of liberty raised by our fathers and cemented by their blood, when its pillars are tottering to their base, of the mean, craven wretches who should begin to quarrel as to who had set it on fire? In God's name let us all unite and put out the flames. It is the temple of our liberty, the nation's house that is on fire, and we call upon every man to do all he can, however little that may be, to avert the danger, and to do it now—to stay this conflagration, and save and transmit to your children, and children's children, this glorious inheritance which we received from our fathers.

Here a large delegation, with banners flying, preceded by a band of music, from the ship-carpenter's department of the United States Navy, made its appearance, bringing a fresh accession of members to the already dense throng in front of the platform. "God Speed the Right" was then given by the Glee Club, with a heartiness and spirit that added greatly to the interest and enthusiasm of the meeting.

SPEECH OF CHARLES GOULD, ESQ.

Mr. GOULD came forward and said:—

FELLOW-CITIZENS,—What is to be the effect of this stupendous gathering of freemen? Let us have one single practical result, which will do us and do our common country good, and we shall not have met in vain. Let us resolve to have this war ended, and ended in the right way; and we shall hear, in less than three months, the magnificent shout of victory swelling from the North to the South, from the Atlantic to the Pacific. We want volunteers, and we want to send them in such a way, and under such orders, as will terminate the war. [A Voice—"Why don't you go yourself?"] I have sent two of my children, and I hope you will all send yours, or go yourselves.

It makes no difference who fights for us, but it makes a great difference who fights against us. If we can get away the supporters, the laborers from the Southern army, we can conquer them at once. Take away their laborers from the fields, and the ditches and embankments. [Great cheering.] Let liberty be by our Government proclaimed to the slaves, and every slave in the South will know the fact. The masters will be compelled to leave the armies of the rebellion and hasten home to protect their property and guard their families; and our army, then tru'y the army of freedom, with hardly the loss of a man, will sweep from Mason and Dixon's line to the Gulf, and the victory for freedom be won and won, forever.

Do you ask how this is to *be* done? The way is simple and easy. Enforce and carry out the proclamation of my friend and your friend here at my side. (Major General Fremont,) and the work *is* done. [Great cheering.]

SPEECH OF COL. JAS. FAIRMAN.

Col. JAS. FAIRMAN was the next speaker. He said:—

FELLOW-CITIZENS,—I will confess that it is under no ordinary degree of embarrassment that I meet you on the present occasion. I have frequently mingled my counsel with yours in the blessed peace of the past, when you and I exulted in being citizens of the Empire City, of the Empire State; contemplating this great city as the apex of a pyramid of civilization and power, whose broad firm base was our continent country.

Who dreamed then—and how brief the interval—that we would be so soon assembled, as at this hour, to gaze with ill-suppressed alarm in each other's faces, to gravely counsel in the desperate necessity of calling from the peaceful channels of industry, nearly a million of men to combat, upon our own soil, the enemies of our laws, liberty, civilization and national existence. Enemies not martialed under a foreign banner, familiar to history, suggesting old feuds and rival systems, with alien languages, institutions and origin ; but men, who but yesterday joined with us in the maintenance and defence, and glorying in the proud significence of that flag, under which, as a united people, we have attained a progress in wealth and power unprecedented in human history, and which is now torn from the staff by Americans, with the red hand of rebellion, in the land of Washington.! Indeed, it is not discreditable to the sagacity of any man to admit that the present aspect of our country amazes and appalls him ; for it would seem that, equally, the motives which govern the best and worst of men, plead against the, not only criminal, but wanton attempt at the destruction of a government which fosters the welfare of its humblest inhabitant, and to whose career the patriots of every clime were wont to look with trembling hope as the auroral light of that day that would usher in the realization of man's highest earthly destiny.

The defence of liberty and laws, even to the shedding of a deluge of human blood, if need be, is the first of rights, though the last of expedients. I therefore feel no need of apology, while claiming to be opposed to the destruction of human life in every instinct of my nature, that I wear a uniform that is significant of sanguinary strife, at a time like the present. For discussion and diplomacy are at an end, and we are left to choose whether we will fight at Richmond or at New-York and Philadelphia. It has come to this, either the Mississippi and the James or the Delaware and the North rivers must bear the crimson tinge which tells to wailing hearts the tale of fraternal strife.

I will speak to you in the spirit of the instruction given by Napoleon to his marshals, when he said, "Send what you please to the bulletins, but tell me the truth." Therefore, while it may not be a welcome announcement, fidelity to my country demands it should be made, that you have held the enemy, heretofore, in unmerited contempt as to their fighting powers. You forget that they are Anglo-Saxons, like yourselves, having every natural element of power that you possess, and in addition, some appliances to awaken their energies, which, I regret to say, are neglected in our own army. And I would here allude to some of the elements which impart to this contest its fearful animus, presenting difficulties, which, did we not know that this rebellion lifts its red hand in sacrilegious defiance against the great whitet hrone of the universe, would well-nigh lead us to despond. The leaders of the South, with a sagacity we would do well to imitate, address the patriotism and passions of their men. There is not an article published in a northern paper, no matter how obscure, which is susceptible of being tortured into an ungenerous or barbarous significance, but it is immediately seized, promulgated and enforced with a fiendish ingenuity of comment, which fans to a savage fury the too susceptible natures of men reared amid an atmosphere which fosters prejudice and arrogance, to the destruction of every feeling of nationality. And to more certainly effect their purpose, the exercise takes the form of a catechism, where the speaker recites some alleged violence to women or children, or something of the kind, by the Union forces, such as the hell-born lie which they fulminated about Butler's proclamation in New Orleans ; and then demanding, " Fathers of the South, will you bear this without a bloody retribution?" Of course there is a thundering " Never !" And the various relations of life are thus appealed to, by exciting interrogatories with the peculiar vehemence of southern elocution, till every element of the human heart joins in the cry for vengeance in the blood of the Union Army. The religion of the south, also, is directed to furnish motives to robbery and murder ; and where it cannot be so directed it is suppressed, and the same iron hand that would shut the ear of humanity against the wail of the bondman, would seek to stifle the breath of prayer, if it could not be impressed into asking the benedictions of the God of justice upon the most flagrant inhumanity and crime that stains the page of human history. And while this demoniacal industry is exerted to poison the mind by the press, the same assiduity is seen in efforts to prevent the communication of intelligence calculated to shake the confidence of the blinded rebels as to their ultimate success. Prisoners brought into our lines within the last two weeks, deny that New Orleans, Memphis, or Nashville are held by Union troops, and tenaciously assert that a Union gunboat cannot pass the guns of Lovell on the Mississippi! And no matter how well a man may know the facts, he dare not, as he values his life, hint that the lies framed for the deception of the masses, are other than the truth they claim.

The palpable, physical elements of this contest, on the part of the enemy, are truly stupendous. The entire population of the South, in a military sense, are impressed into the service ; every kind of property in the rebel States which can be used for any military purpose, is seized ; and the sole hope of replevin, is predicated upon the permanence of the Confederate government. The entire currency of these States is dependent for its redemption upon the success of the rebellion ; while they now hold ample territory with abundant natural resources for an empire, and awaiting only the ever precarious caprices of European diplomacy for foreign recognition with the practical sympathy annexed.

My past, I trust, preserves me from suspicion of disloyalty while I thus speak of the power of the rebels ; and I believe it is best to be frank, even if it should savor of compliment, as the first thing toward a successful contest is to squarely face the enemy. Then let me add, what is the fruit of ample opportunities of knowledge, as my conviction, that until the power of this rebellion is crushed with a gauntlet hand, you cannot call the ground upon which you now stand either free or independent ; for, chimerical as it may seem to you, still the scheme is entertained with a lively hope by the rebels, of invading the cities of New-York and Philadelphia, to repay with their plunder the losses incurred by the desolation of Virginia ; and while you repose in a security, based upon the vast population and resources of these cities, you must remember, that military success depends in some cases entirely upon organization. Ridgeley, in his account of Buena Vista, says, there were Mexicans enough to bind every American and carry him into Mexico, but they lacked organization ; and to those familiar with military operations it does not look like phantasy altogether. (in the absence of energetic action on the part of the North.) when we hear the apparently wild menace of the rebels dictating peace before the walls of Philadelphia and New-York. Thus I have glanced briefly at the elements, strength, and purposes of the rebel conspiracy. I have purposely refrained from the discussion of the agencies which contributed to bring this scourge upon us as a people. I feel, however, constrained to state one fact, elicited from a variety of sources—namely, that the course of some of the public men of the North, in the past, has inspired the rebels with the conviction that they have allies in the North, whose overt co-operation is only prevented by fears of mob violence, and who, at the sight of the three barred flag would break the union of that North which now brings pallor to the cheek of treason. And at different times, while urging intelligent rebels by the terrors of the national arm, and pleading with fraternal earnestness in view of the traditions of the glorious old Flag; to induce them to abandon the heresy and crime of secession, I have been met with the speeches, resolutions, and platforms of Northern political leaders, giving promises to justify every claim of the rebels even to bloody isolation, as a remedy for the alleged wrongs of the South ; and this blighting stultification paralyzes even now, in a great measure, all attempts to convince the rebels that the North and nation are verily in earnest.

These are some of the facts in view of which we must act. If any man doubted that we are fighting practically an aroused nation, the march from Fortress Monroe to Richmond, presenting seventy miles of desolated homesteads and abandoned plantations, is calculated to correct and convince him. And under the views and information to which the mass of the rebels are limited, they, doubtless, earnestly believe, that the war in which they are engaged is as righteous, justifiable, and hopeful as that of the Revolution of '76.

In view of these facts, then, it is not simply an expedient, subject to our discretion, *which way* to use to put down the rebellion; for it is patent to the humblest understanding, that an earnest purpose to put down rebellion will be indicated by using *every* instrumentality calculated to compass that end. If this be so, then, how are we to understand a discussion of three weeks' duration, as to whether it would not be better to *prohibit by law*, the use of loyal men of a particular shade in quelling this rebellion. The arguments adverse to the employment of blacks being silenced by the Battle of New Orleans, and more emphatically so, by the operations in Hayti in the attempt to re-enslave that people—when the negroes, under the leadership of a man born a slave, hurled the disciplined troops of two of the most warlike nations of Europe, quivering from their shores; when only by a meanly contrived stratagem of the great Napoleon, and by it getting the person of L'Overture in his power, could France temporarily subdue the little island of Hayti. I am not advocating either the social or political rights of any race, adversely. I prefer to speak on one subject at a time, and I speak of the muscles of a black man as I would of the muscles of a horse, for a definite purpose; and, in my opinion, nothing can transcend the beetle-headed stupidity of those men, who cannot discuss the digging of trenches and shooting of rifles without merging, by an affinity of ideas known only to themselves, into the most occult questions of ethnology, as to essential equalities of races, etc. How absurd it would seem if we stood in " Fives Court," London, about a century ago, while Cribb and Moleneaux were contending for the championship of England, and would there suggest the essential difference of the white and black races as a settlement of the question contested by the two giants. It will be remembered that on that occasion the black was beaten by *foul play*—a thing of which the negro seems to have always had his share. I would suggest to these philosophers that we do not stick to purity of races in the army now. A mule compared to a horse would be considered a rather illegitimate style of an animal, yet nothing but mules could pull long enough and fast enough to suit our recent march to the James River, notwithstanding the inferiority of the race. But, seriously, I would here make a remark which I will not allow my shoulder-straps to suppress; shoulder-straps or no shoulder-straps, I say that I have seen men suffering the privations inseparable from the line of duty during the recent campaign on the Isthmus, doing a hard day's duty in the field, followed by a hard tour of duty in digging trenches, and human nature has sunk beneath the load, and I have seen them rolled in their blanket and laid down in their final rest—superinduced, doubtless, by a tax upon their energies which might have been divided with the slave, who must, inevitably, share the benefit of the triumph. I leave the transcendental philosophers to defend that policy which sacrifices a white man to save a black one, while at the same time, contending for the superiority of the former. Let every man who claims to be a patriot banish his theories of the past, and suspend his schemes for the future, wherever they would interfere with present usefulness. We are now at war with the rebels, *we are now at war with the rebels;* therefore, all words and acts indicating any other treatment of the rebellion than by the sword, is treason or imbecility. When war begins, diplomacy is exhausted. That man is simply a knave who speaks of conciliation while the red tide of blood dyes the banks of the James and the Chickahominy. The two policies of combating and conciliation cannot be at the same time pursued by the Government. And it is a still bolder treason and fraud to suppose that they can be both applied by a general in the field. It would seem in the past, as if some of our generals thought *Civil War*, meant a war conducted without giving offence to the enemy. And some have secured the applause of the enemy by *olive branch campaigns* and *conciliatory conflicts!* Let the line be drawn at once, and let those who still chirp conciliation seek the purlieus of putrid politics, and let not the "tainted rebel stain the soldier." I here utter an apothegm, and recommend to rigid application; whenever a general has become popular with the enemy, it is time that we were done with him. The American Nation mean to conquer treason, and will view as enemies those who stand between them and the foes of our flag. We cannot conquer without being deeply in earnest; for our enemy is determined, numerous, and brave, and your superior numbers and resources will not save you unless you bring them to bear.

No man will think lightly of this contest, who stood, as I did, at Fair Oaks, and saw the enemy for six hours pour their masses into the very jaws of death; for I saw them march boldly into the open field, as near as the outskirts of this assemblage, where every discharge of our cannon marked a deep gulf in the advancing mass, who still advanced, literally over heaps of the dead, till that bloody arena was so covered with prostrate confederates, till at nightfall, it was like a ghastly bivouac, terribly significant of the desperate energy of the rebellion.

Yet we will triumph! I feel assured in saying this, from the evidence of my senses, of the indomitable valor of the individual soldier in the Union ranks. And I will confess to some surprise at the bravery and efficiency of mere boys on the battle-field. I saw young Americans in the Union ranks, so light and frail, as to preclude their acceptance as soldiers, having been mustered as drummers, shoulder rifles and rush into the fight, loading and firing with a rapidity and tact, that brought many a brown uniform to the dust. And when, after a conflict of over six hours' duration, in various duties and parts of the field, I found myself surrounded by nine members of my command, whose devotion found expression in voluntarily remaining by my side, two of the nine were drummer-boys, their faces begrimed with powder, but lit up with an inspiration that showed they felt the majesty of their mission. How can such an army be finally conquered? Is there not a sublimity in that comparatively little band of Spartans making a Thermopylæ of Harrison's Bar, and holding their clinched hands in defiance at the rebel hosts around them. Shall these men cry in vain for a sufficient number to join their decimated ranks, to give them a proximate equality of numbers for the last grand contest, where all the hopes of our hearts are at stake? Is not this blood too precious to shed in contests where nothing is determined, except to show the world that our country is a nation of soldiers?

Then promptly furnish the three hundred thousand bayonets that will end this contest with the lasting triumph of Liberty and Union. And my word for it, that if this be promptly done the cadence of three hundred thousand marching on the rebel capital will shake with their earthquake tread the centre of the rebellion, and there will be no more battles in the sense of Pittsburg Landing, Fort Donelson, Fair Oaks, and the contests of the last two weeks. Then what we want is, that you, your fathers, brothers, friends, join in every movement calculated to haste the consummation by a rapid reinforcement of the army on the James River. Let no man or boy who can bear a rifle mistake or neglect his duty in this hour of our country's peril. In this great contest there is not a man in this broad land so humble as to be removed from the consequences of the issue.

I have sometimes, while pacing outside of my tent under the beautiful starlight of a Virginia sky, the quiet and darkness inspiring a reflective mood, tried to grasp the momentous interests involved in this struggle. I have looked in imagination into the dark gulf of disintegration and ruin upon the verge of which our country seemed to stand upon a trembling base, and contemplated the possibility of the splendid temple of our Liberties and Nationality broken into as many conflicting fragments as there are States and Territories, with rival interests, institutions, policies and prejudices, proscriptive passports, postage and commercial laws, contiguous territory and consequent necessities for ponderous military establishments, with the perpetual danger and tendency of a combination of a portion against the remainder, and the temptation to foreign invasion, till, with rapid pace and throbbing brow, I have wondered if these reflections are a secret, or how men can be so dead in the midst of a storm so portentous.

Then let us be admonished, and know that national existence, liberty, order, law, the organization of human society upon a civilized basis, and the vast charge given us by our fathers for posterity, signified in the star-spangled emblem of the brotherhood of freemen—all tremble in precarious existence, so long as there is upon the continent a pole on end with the three-barred ensign of treason and murder upon it. And let us not only bring to a bloody grave this monster of our day, but let us bring our children, like young Hannibals, to the altar of our country, and from their infant lips extort the obligation that will doom the man whose temerity leads him to the remotest sympathy with the foul instigators of this hideous drama.

The whites of the South plead, by the circumstances to which I have hurriedly alluded, for deliverance; for a large portion of the passion and patriotism now swelling the rebellion would, by the power of a free press and an honest pulpit, be converted to the cause of the Union. But you must remember that the iron arm which now grasps the throat of press and pulpit in the rebel States, must be broken with the sword before you can inaugurate these remedial measures. A free press and an honest pulpit cannot precede your arms, but can only come on the heel of rifled cannon and Federal bayonets.

Then let us show how we prize our liberties by alacrity in their defence; let us not be stingy of blood where it will bring such large revenue of blessings to our country and the human race. And doing our duty in this dark hour, we will sustain that flag whose folds are radiant with glorious memories of the past, with all its proud significance intensified by the struggle, and see our country rise from this bloody baptism into a new life and majesty as truly the land of the FREE and the home of the BRAVE. We will triumph the moment we deserve to. Then let us vindicate on the field our sincerity when we say,—

"Forever float that standard sheet,
Where breathes the foe but falls before us?
With freedom's soil beneath our feet,
And freedom's banner floating o'er us."

SPEECH OF COLONEL SIMON H. MIX.

Colonel SIMON H. MIX, of the Second New-York cavalry, Burnside's expedition, came forward, and was greeted with cheers. He spoke as follows:—

My fellow-citizens, it is the duty of a soldier at all times to fight. [A voice, "We know that."] It is sometimes the duty of a soldier to speak. I consider this as one of those occasions; for inasmuch as I am incapacitated from doing the former, through the politeness of an invitation extended to me by your committee, I shall try my hand at the latter. It seems to me, my fellow-citizens, but a day since I left the city of New-York to go to the battle-field. Almost the last day I spent in this city was on the occasion of a great monster meeting in this Square, held about eighteen months ago. I then resolved to go to the interior of the State, from whence I came, and appeal to the Union men there and raise a cavalry regiment, and I did not appeal in vain. My friends, I wish to say here distinctly that I am not here for the purpose of criticising any of the acts of my superiors. With the man who is placed over me will I serve and fight at all times. [Vociferous cheering.] I have served under Gen. McClellan. [Here three cheers were given for Gen. McClellan.] I have served under Gen. Banks —[cheers]—I have served under the great and glorious Burnside. [Great cheering.] In this connection I wish to say a word. Experience is the best teacher, and when any man comes to you and tells you if the negroes of the South are employed in the army the soldiers that we have there will not fight, do you tell that man he is a fool, and that he does not know what he is talking about. [Great cheering.] In the South they have what we term farmers by day and soldiers by night ; rebel bandits, who prowl around and shoot down our soldiers upon the outposts. Only yesterday, when I came from Newbern, I brought several soldiers of my regiment who had suffered in that way. I would take the negroes of the South and put muskets in their hands, for nowhere in the swamps of North Carolina can you find a path where a dog can go that the negro does not understand. There are gentlemen here who will bear me witness when I state this fact, that in all our expeditions in North Carolina we have depended upon the negroes for our guides ; for without them we could not have moved with any safety The information we have received from them has always been reliable and always correct. I have never known an instance to the contrary. [Applause.] My friends, you all no doubt wonder how it is that the South has arrayed in front of the Federal army at Richmond two hundred thousand men. But it can be easily explained. Every man in the South who can carry a shot-gun, had, of necessity to become a soldier. There are two classes in the South—the representative men, who number fifteen or twenty in a county, and the poor whites. if you throw out of the account the blacks ; but so far as my observation extends, the blacks are a much superior class in intellect to the poor degraded whites of the South. What is done with these poor whites ? They are dragged ruthlessly from their homes, and compelled to go into the army. When I first reached Newbern, the duty was assigned to me to advance into the country thirty miles on each side, over ground that our troops had not before then occupied. Wherever I went I found houses deserted, and the mothers, wives and children weeping for those who had been taken from their homes and carried to the army.

I hold in my hand a scrap of paper, from *The Raleigh Standard*, which contains the following :—

HEAD-QUARTERS N. C. MILITIA, ADJUTANT-GENERAL'S OFFICE,
RALEIGH, *Dec.* 21*st*, 1861.

SPECIAL ORDER NO. 77.—Lieut. Sanford Earnest, of the 71st Regiment N. C. Militia, having declared his preference for the Government of the United States, and having declined to march under the flag of the Confederate States, is hereby dismissed, being unworthy of a commission in the Militia of the State—and will hereafter do duty as a private.

The Colonel will have this order read before the Regiment, and printed in the newspapers of his county.

By order of the Commander-in-Chief,

J. G. MARTIN, *Adjutant-General.*

That is the way they are treated. [Cries of "Shame, shame!"]

The Colonel proceeded to give some further incidents connected with his experiences while in North Carolina, which were listened to with great interest, but brought his speech abruptly to a close—the rain, which came up so suddenly, having already began to fall, and causing the hasty dispersion of a large portion of the immense throng.

At this juncture a rain-storm set in and rendered an adjournment absolutely necessary; but previous to separating, FRANK W. BALLARD moved, and CEPHAS BRAINERD seconded, the following resolutions, which were adopted:—

Resolved, That the young men of New-York, alive to the exigencies of the crisis now upon the country, and, as ever, devoted to the preservation of the pure democratic principle, are bound by every interest to press forward into the ranks, and, in the most earnest, speedy, and effectual manner, put an end *forever* to the accursed idea of Secession and Disunion. To us life is valueless without Liberty, Liberty useless without Union, and Union merely nominal if the idea of Secession is not finally and forever put to sleep, beyond an awakening this side of Hell.

Resolved, That, while we have no sympathy with any class of demagogues who place conditions upon their professions of loyalty to the Union, we are sensible that our army is waging this war with fettered hands, and we beseech this Government to overstep the constructive bounds which prevent the employment of *every*, EVERY, EVERY means of suppressing this infernal rebellion.

The Committee of Arrangements and the public were indebted to Major WILLARD of the Anthon Battery of Light Artillery, and to Messrs. BREWSTER & Co. and the workmen of their manufactory, for the salutes which were fired at stated periods during the proceedings

Their thanks are also due to the gentlemen who kindly volunteered their services as a Chorus, and who added so much to the interest of the proceedings.

They were Messrs. Henry Camp, Sigismund Lasar, F. G. Taylor, Charles Loomis, Henry Molten, Geo. N. Seymour, Joseph B. Mather, John J. Ennis, E. G. Bartlett, Geo. E. Aiken, Jonathan Aiken, Charles Aiken, Henry J. Wright, and Messrs. Anderson and Deyo.

INVITATION TO DISTINGUISHED CITIZENS TO ADDRESS THE MEETING OF LOYAL CITIZENS.

NEW YORK, *July* 11*th*, 1862.

SIR,—At a Convention of Committees, severally appointed by the Common Council of this city, by the Chamber of Commerce of the State of New-York, by the Union Defence Committee, and by bodies of Loyal Citizens of this city, it was resolved to hold, on Tuesday, the 15th instant, a Mass Meeting of all parties who are in favor of supporting the Government in the prosecution of the war and suppressing the rebellion, and to express, without reference to any party question whatever, their undiminished confidence in the justice of the cause, and their inflexible determination to sustain it; and to that end to proffer to the Government their aid to the extent of all their resources.

In accordance with this purpose, the undersigned were appointed by the Convention a Committee to invite distinguished citizens, of all parties, to address the meeting upon its object, and in the spirit in which it is convened.

In performance of this duty, it affords us much pleasure to request that you will address the meeting on that occasion. Be pleased to give us your acceptance of this invitation, by note, addressed to the Secretary of this Committee, at the Chamber of Commerce, as soon as convenient.

JAMES W. WHITE,
GEO. OPDYKE,
SAMUEL SLOAN,
PROSPER M. WETMORE,
DENNING DUER,
CHARLES GOULD,
} *Select Committee.*

CHAS. GOULD, *Secretary.*

GENTLEMEN INVITED TO ADDRESS THE MEETING.

Hon. Hannibal Hamlin,
Hon. William H. Seward, ⎫
Hon. Salmon P. Chase, ⎪
Hon. Edwin M. Stanton, ⎬ *Cabinet.*
Hon. Gideon Welles, ⎪
Hon. Montgomery Blair, ⎪
Hon. Edward Bates, ⎪
Hon. Caleb B. Smith, ⎭
Gov. Edwin D. Morgan,
Gov. John A. Andrew,
Gov. Israel Washburn, Jr.,
Gov. N. S. Berry,
Gov. Frederick Holbrook,
Gov. William A. Buckingham,
Gov. Charles S. Olden,
Gov. A. G. Curtin,
Gov. A. W. Bradford,
Gov. F. H. Peirpont,
Gov. Austin Blair,
Gov. Andrew Johnson,
Gov. H. R. Gamble,
Gov. O. P. Morton,
Gov. David Todd,
Gov. Alexander Ramsey,
Gov. Richard Yates,
Gov. Edward Salomon,
Gov. William Sprague,
Hon. Lot M. Morrill,
Hon. William P. Fessenden,
Hon. John P. Hale,
Hon. Preston King,
Hon. Ira Harris,
Hon. John Sherman,
Hon. Benj. F. Wade,
Hon. David Wilmot,
Hon. H. B. Anthony,
Hon. Solomon Foot,
Hon. Jacob Collamer,
Hon. Charles Sumner,
Hon. Henry Wilson,
Hon. Zachariah Chandler,
Hon. J. W. Grimes,
Hon. Lyman Trumbull,
Hon. Henry M. Rice,
Hon. M. S. Wilkinson,
Hon. J. B. Henderson,
Hon. Joseph A. Wright,
Hon. Moses F. Odell,
Hon. William Wall,
Hon. Alfred Ely,
Hon. Daniel S. Dickinson,
Hon. Edward Haight,
Hon. Frederick A. Conkling,
Hon. Schuyler Colfax,
Hon. Owen Lovejoy,
Hon. John F. Potter,
Hon. Elijah Ward,
Hon. Roscoe Conkling,
Hon. Galusha A. Grow,
Hon. Francis P. Blair, Jr.,
Hon. Henry L. Dawes,
Hon. Elisha B. Washburne,
Hon. Lyman Tremaine,
Hon. Richard B. Connolly,
Hon. George Bancroft,
Hon. Horace Binney,
Hon. Edward Everett,
Hon. John A. King,
Hon. Joseph Holt,
Hon. Carl Shulz,
Gen. Hiram Walbridge,
John W. Forney, Esq.,
William Curtis Noyes, Esq.,
Maj. Gen'l John C. Fremont, U. S. A.
David Dudley Field, Esq.,
Com. Andrew H. Foote,
Richard Busteed, Esq.,
William M. Evarts, Esq.,
James T. Brady, Esq.,
Francis B. Cutting, Esq.,
Charles King, Esq.,
Rev. Dr. H. W. Bellows,
Rev. Dr. R. W. Hitchcock,
Rev. Dr. Vinton,
Rev. W. G. Brownlow,
Rev. Henry Ward Beecher,
Rev. J. P. Thompson,
Major Gen'l John E. Wool,
Brig. Gen'l Franz Sigel,
Brig. Gen'l Shields,
Brig. Gen. S. Van Vliet,
General Lewis Wallace,
Col. Francis B. Spinola,
Judge Chas. P. Daly,
Prof. A. D. Bache,
Lieut. Gen'l Winfield Scott,
Major Gen'l John A. Dix,
Major Gen'l James S. Wadsworth,
Major Charles W. Le Gendre,
Brig. Gen'l John Cochrane,
Brig. Gen'l O. M. Mitchell,
Judge Edwards Pierrepont,
Frederick Kapp, Esq.,
Orestes A. Brownson, Esq.,
L. E. Chittenden, Esq.,
D. S. Coddington, Esq.,
James A. Briggs, Esq.,
George Gibbs, Esq.
Hon. W. H. Wallace.

REPLIES OF DISTINGUISHED CITIZENS.

LETTER FROM WILLIAM H. SEWARD, SECRETARY OF STATE.

DEPARTMENT OF STATE, }
WASHINGTON, 14th July, 1862. }

*To James W. White, George Opdyke, and others, Esquires,
Select Committee, &c.:*

GENTLEMEN,—Your note, inviting me to attend a meeting of loyal citizens of New-York, to be held to-morrow evening, has been received.

The objects of the meeting are of vital importance. They involve nothing less than a choice between an early peace, with the deliverance of the nation from all surrounding dangers, or a protracted war, with hazards of ultimate national dissolution.

Public duties forbid my leaving the Capital at this moment; but I have given to the only male member of my family, not already in the public service, permission to enroll himself as a private in the ranks of the volunteers, which it is your purpose to send into the field.

I have the honor to be, gentlemen,

Your very obedient servant,

WILLIAM H. SEWARD.

LETTER OF E. D. MORGAN, GOVERNOR OF STATE OF NEW-YORK.

STATE OF NEW-YORK, EXECUTIVE DEPARTMENT, }
ALBANY, *July* 14th, 1862. }

GENTLEMEN :

I have received your invitation to be present and address the mass meeting of the citizens of New-York, on Union Square, to-morrow afternoon, for the purpose of expressing their undiminished confidence in the justice of our cause, and to proffer to the Government their aid, to the *extent of their resources*.

I feel that this gathering will be worthy the occasion which calls it forth, worthy the great city whose potential voice has more than once given encouragement to the Government and country in the dark hours of this struggle—a meeting that will be remembered in after-time, as an index of the mighty spirit that moved the people of 1862, to declare anew that the Union "must and shall be preserved."

The preliminary work of enlistment, just now, seems to demand my presence here, and I shall, therefore, be unable to meet with you to-morrow. But my interest will be in no degree abated because of my absence, for I feel that the action of New-York at this time is a matter of the deepest importance. Let the great metropolis of the country again emphatically declare its purpose to uphold the cause of the Union to the last, by giving of its men and means, if necessary, "to the extent of its resources," and it will arouse the whole country. Already meetings are appointed for the same evening as your own. This capital and other cities will have their masses in council at the same hour that you are collected together. Here, as in New-York and elsewhere, matters of mere political policy are, as they should be, forgotten, and partisan clamor hushed, in view of the country's peril. Let us, for the present at least, only remember that we are fellow-members of a commonwealth. Let us show that in the hour of danger we can rise superior to the prejudices of the past, and together prepare to defend, successfully, the "palladium of our political safety and happiness."

A period has come when none can hesitate, none can be idle. In the providence of God, it would seem that before the evil cloud shall pass, all must be brought to sacrifice something for the country's cause; either to render personal service in the field, furnish material aid, or assume the care of families of volunteers. So much is duty. Let it be done, and done quickly. In perilous times, delay is treason. The necessities of our situation are inevitable. The questions presented are terribly practical. Men are the want of the hour. Our State will respond to the call of the President; but to assure this, the families of volunteers must be provided for. While fighting for fireside rights, their own firesides, in their absence, must not be permitted to be darkened by want. If the response to the requisition is promptly made, we may expect increased vigor in putting down the rebellion and vindicating the national power, and that blows quick and heavy shall be made to fall upon the staggering forces of the insurgents. All the powers possessed by the leaders of the rebellion are being used by them with passionate zeal. Let us, then, ask that they be met with at least equal earnestness by the National Government. Longer lenity to rebels is rank injustice to loyal men.

I have the honor to be, with great respect,
Your obedient servant,
E. D. MORGAN.

To JAMES W. WHITE, Esq. Hon. GEO. OPDYKE, Hon. SAMUEL SLOAN, PROSPER M. WETMORE, Esq., DENNING DUER, Esq., CHARLES GOULD, Esq., *Committee*.

LETTER OF F. H. PEIRPOINT, GOV. OF VIRGINIA.

EXECUTIVE CHAMBER, WHEELING, VA., }
July 16*th*, 1862.   }

James W. White, George Opdyke, Samuel Sloan, and others, N. Y.:

GENTLEMEN,—Your favor requesting me to address a meeting of the citizens of New-York, composed of all persons, without distinction of party, who are in favor of prosecuting the war and suppressing the rebellion, is received. The delay of the mail in bringing your request in time, if no other cause, prevents my being with you. I would like to be there. The heart of every true patriot will respond to the object of the meeting with a joyful Amen.

New-York now occupies a position second to no other city in the world. She controls the finances and commerce of the continent. Your city is one of the triumphs of American freedom. Put down the rebellion, establish free schools, a free press and free speech in the Southern States, and New-York's present is only the beginning of her future greatness. It is right that such movement should commence there.

You say the object of the meeting is "to express, without reference to any party question whatever, your undiminished confidence in the justice of the cause, and your inflexible determination to sustain it; and, to that end, to proffer to the Government your aid, to the extent of all your resources."

Gentlemen these words have the ring of the pure metal. They will gladden the throbbing heart of the nation. What patriot will stop at this hour of his country's peril to cavil about party? Be sure that we have a *country* to govern, before we begin the contest who shall govern it. The cup of our political sins will not be drained, until we can look *beyond* party to our country, and our country only.

Six months before the breaking out of the rebellion, all that portion of our country outside of the rebel States was the most prosperous and happy people on the face of the earth. But the rebels, like Haman, borne down by the weight of their own impotency, envious of their more prosperous neighbors, conceived the scheme of taking from us, by inaugurating this rebellion, the glorious inheritance of our fathers, purchased by their blood freely spilled upon an hundred battle-fields. We owe it to ourselves, to posterity, to the sacred memory of our fathers, to mete to them Haman's fate. To do this, we should be as economical as possible of the lives of the loyal soldiers, and provide bountifully for those going to the field and for those they leave behind.

Say to them when they go, "Use all the means God and nature and circumstances have put in your power to suppress the rebellion and punish traitors." Rebels' property, in the rebel sense of the word, of whatever kind, sensible or insensible, should be made to contribute to the suppression of the rebellion in any manner that it can be made available.

This war has been inaugurated and prosecuted by the rebels without reference to the rights of Union men. It is not for them to claim constitutional guaranties. They have no rights under the Constitution, save the infliction of the penalty of their crimes. They have grown insolent by their dominion over their own slaves, until they have adopted as their political axiom, "that Slavery is the normal condition of the working classes." Upon that principle they are attempting to build their empire. This is in derogation of English liberty and American liberty, and of all that has raised the Anglo-Saxon race to its present greatness in this country and in Europe. It is an attempt to degrade every free laboring man in the nation ; not only the native born, but the German and Irishman, who seek an asylum in this land of the free, are denounced as only fit for slaves.

Mr. Jefferson has given us advice intended, doubtless, for occasions like the present. He says :—"A strict observance of the written law is, doubtless, one of the highest duties of a good citizen.. ; but not the highest. The law of necessity of self-preservation, of saving our country when in danger, are of higher obligation. To lose our country by a scrupulous adherence to written law, would be to lose the law itself, with life, liberty, property, and all those who are enjoying them with us ; thus absurdly sacrificing the end to the means." Here is a chart made for the occasion by one who comprehended our institutions and the enormities of rebellion.

Gentlemen, this is the last contest our free institutions will have, if we put forth the strength of the nation, and punish rebellion as it deserves. But remember, there is but *one* time left to put down the usurpers—that is *the present*. We cannot fold our arms this year, and fight the next. We must fight *now*, or all is lost. The contest is gigantic—the result, the freedom or enslavement of the nation. It is the removal of the last fetter thrown around the thirteen old colonies. Redeemed and disenthralled, America will rise with new strength, and in sublime proportions, the beauty of the whole earth.

This is the most gigantic rebellion the world ever saw. There is the most gigantic stake being played for. The question is : *Shall Slavery or Freedom be universal?* There is no concealing it. This is the issue. The rebels have presented and *forced* it upon the nation. We have accepted, and it is to be tried at the point of the bayonet and the muzzle of the cannon : and were it not for the traitors in our midst, the verdict for freedom would be rendered in three months. Every device that the devil can invent and put into the heads of traitors, seems to be brought forward to keep men out of the field, and to paralyze the arms of those already there. These traitors are tolerated in high and low places. It is the grasp of their hand now upon the body politic that partially paralyzes our strength. They are endeavoring to enlarge their grasp. This is our danger. But there were traitors in the camp of Moses, in the social family of Jesus Christ ; in the army of the Revolution, and it would be wonderful if we had them not now in this our country's struggle. They have ever received their reward, and they will, doubtless, in the present instance.

Gentlemen, everything depends on prompt, resolute and determined action, under the blessing of God.

          I am, yours, &c.,   F. H. PEIRPOINT.

LETTER OF ISRAEL WASHBURN, JR., GOVERNOR OF MAINE.

STATE OF MAINE, EXECUTIVE DEPARTMENT,
AUGUSTA, *July* 12*th*, 1862.

Charles Gould, Esq.:

DEAR SIR,—I have received your invitation to take part in a meeting of the faithful citizens of New-York, to be held on the 15th instant. While on that day I can serve the cause, in the interest of which the meeting is called, only by attending to the duties which crowd upon me here, my heart and hopes will be with the good and earnest men who will come together at that time in the vast metropolis, to speak to the American people of the demands and necessities of the hour. The country is in danger, but it can and must be saved. Let the people but perceive the greatness and imminence of the peril, and they will rise to the height of every sacrifice that is required of them. Never before were they so appealed to by all that is strongest and noblest in manly hearts. The necessity is upon them to fight for their homes, for honor, and for life. Let the coward blanch if he must; let the faint-hearted fail in the hour of his country's agony, and let the miscreant traitor consent that this fair heritage—all the gains of all the ages—the hope of future generations, of the millions yet to be—liberty, civilization, "the thousand years of peace"—all, all, shall be cast away and lost, utterly and forever—the true and patriotic men will unite in one earnest, resolute, devoted, and successful effort to crush out a revolt so causeless and wicked as to whiten by the contrast all previous crimes in the history of nations.

The struggle must be short, sharp and decisive; for in a war like this, temporizing is waste, and timidity is cruelty. Every lawful expedient and means which the Government can lay hold of, to put down this rebellion, must be used; and every man in the country, without respect to race or complexion, who can aid in this work, must be employed for the sake of every other man.

Your meeting is called, primarily, to arouse the country to the duties of the crisis; and so certain is it to accomplish this end, that it may assure the Administration at Washington, that if this Government is to be broken up, it will not be by reason of any neglect or fault of the people.

I have the honor to be, very truly,
Your obedient servant,
ISRAEL WASHBURN, JR.

LETTER OF CHARLES S. OLDEN, GOVERNOR OF NEW JERSEY.

STATE OF NEW JERSEY, EXECUTIVE DEPARTMENT,
TRENTON, *July* 14*th*, 1862.

GENTLEMEN:

I have duly received your invitation to attend a meeting of the citizens of New-York, to be held on the 15th inst. My official duties are so pressing and incessant that I am compelled to decline it.

At such a time as this it is the plain duty of every citizen to devote his time, his money, and his influence to the support of the Government; if it is not now sustained, our property, our lives, and our liberties are at the mercy of treasonable and dissolute factions.

The influence of your city upon the public sentiment of the country is justly great. The patriotic action of the proposed meeting of your citizens, while it will be highly appreciated by the Government, will produce the most favorable effect among the people, by cheering the patriotic, encouraging the timid, and awing the disloyal.

With great respect, your obedient servant,
CHARLES S. OLDEN.

Messrs. JAMES W. WHITE, GEO. OPDYKE, and others, *Select Committee.*

LETTER OF A. W. BRADFORD, GOVERNOR OF MARYLAND.

STATE OF MARYLAND, EXECUTIVE DEPARTMENT,
ANNAPOLIS, *July* 14*th*, 1862.

Hon. James W. White, George Opdyke, and others, Committee, &c.

GENTLEMEN,—I am honored with your invitation, just received, to attend and address a mass meeting, to-morrow evening, in your city, of "all parties who are in favor of supporting the Government in the prosecution of the war," &c.

My own engagements at present, connected chiefly with objects similar to those contemplated by your Convention, and particularly in promoting by all possible means a prompt response to the late call for volunteers, will, much to my regret, compel me to forego the pleasure of attending your meeting.

With my most cordial wishes for your complete success, and the speedy accomplishment of the object we have in common at heart, .

I am, with great respect,
Your obedient servant,
A. W. BRADFORD.

LETTER OF RICHARD YATES, GOVERNOR OF ILLINOIS.

STATE OF ILLINOIS, EXECUTIVE DEPARTMENT,
SPRINGFIELD, *July* 22*d*, 1862.

Charles Gould, Esq., Sec'y, &c , New-York City:

SIR,—Your invitation to attend the Union mass meeting in your city, on the 15th inst., did not reach me until that day.

It would have afforded me much pleasure to have met the patriotic citizens of the Empire State on that occasion, and interchange with them views upon the conduct of the war, and the best means to be employed in bringing it to a speedy and successful issue.

I am, very respectfully, &c.,
RICHARD YATES,
Gov. of Illinois.

LETTER OF WILLIAM A. BUCKINGHAM, GOVERNOR OF CONNECTICUT.

STATE OF CONNECTICUT, EXECUTIVE DEPARTMENT,
NORWICH, *July* 14*th*, 1862.

Charles Gould, Esq., &c.:

SIR,—Your favor of the 11th inst. is at hand, inviting me to attend, on the 15th inst., a meeting of all parties who are in favor of supporting the Government and suppressing the rebellion.

While public duties will detain me in this State, I beg leave to assure you of my cordial approval of the object of the meeting, and my undiminished confidence that the citizens of this Commonwealth will ever be found co-operating with those of other States, in support of the Government, and that, under God, they will be successful in rescuing it from the power of the rebels, restore peace, and secure a higher degree of civil liberty than we have hitherto enjoyed.

I am, very respectfully, your obedient servant,
WM. A. BUCKINGHAM.

LETTER OF A. G. CURTIN, GOVERNOR OF PENNSYLVANIA.

EXECUTIVE CHAMBER,
HARRISBURG, PA., *July 15th* 1862.

GENTLEMEN :

My duties here will prevent me from being present at your meeting in New-York to-morrow, at which I should have been glad, if circumstances had permitted me, to assist.

Pennsylvania has shown by her conduct how heartily she sympathizes with her sister loyal States. Our people regard this rebellion as a vile treason, devoid of all excuse or palliation, the hideous offspring of the malignity and spite which bad men in inferior and semi barbarous societies entertain against communities which have surpassed them in all the elements of comfort, welfare and civilization. I think the popular mind is fixed in the belief, that the one great present need is a due appreciation by our Government of the fact, that we are at war, and that it is its duty to use all the means for success which are recognized by the established laws of war, and especially to use freely for military purposes every man on the soil of the rebellious States who is willing to serve us. It is silly to waste our resources in the mere parade of war ; we can arrive at no good result if that course be longer pursued.

Repeating the expression of my regret at being unable to assist at your patriotic assemblage,

I am, gentlemen,

Your obedient servant,

A. G. CURTIN.

LETTER OF PRESTON KING, SENATOR FROM NEW-YORK.

WASHINGTON, *July* 12*th*, 1862.

Messrs. James White, Geo. Opdyke, and others:

GENTLEMEN,—Your invitation to me to address a mass meeting of all parties who are in favor of supporting the Government, in the prosecution of the war and suppressing the rebellion, to be held in the city of New-York, on Tuesday, the 15th instant, is received. My whole heart is in the cause your meeting is called to promote, and I wish I could be there, but public engagements here, that I cannot put aside, prevent my attendance. I thank you for the invitation.

Very respectfully,

PRESTON KING.

LETTER OF LOT M. MORRILL, SENATOR FROM MAINE.

SENATE CHAMBER, WASHINGTON, *July* 14*th*, 1862.

GENTLEMEN:

By your favor of the 11th instant, I am informed that, "at a Convention of Committees, severally appointed by the Common Council of this city ; by the Chamber of Commerce of the State of New-York ; by the Union Defence Committee; and by bodies of loyal citizens of this city, it was resolved to hold, on Tuesday, the 15th instant, a mass meeting of all parties who are in favor of supporting the Government in the prosecution of the war, and suppressing the rebellion, and to express, without reference to any party question whatever, their undiminished confidence in the justice of the cause, and their inflexible determination to sustain it, and to that end to proffer to the government their aid to the extent of all their resources ;" and am invited to be present "to address the meeting upon its objects, and in the spirit in which it is convened."

While official duties here compel me to decline the invitation, I cannot forbear the expression, in a brief note, of my unqualified commendation of the spirit and purpose of such a *resolution*, emanating from such a source. In this hour of peril, the country will hail it with exultation ; its lofty purpose and sentiment of patriotic devotion, will reanimate every loyal heart throughout the land. Assailed by a malignant domestic enemy, and menaced by " the malcontent and desperate " everywhere, the Government requires from all its friends, what you generously tender—unconditional and unwavering support, " in the prosecution of the war and suppressing the rebellion." As no government was ever so beneficent, so liberal, so just, so none ever had such claims for support. Self-preservation, the dictates of prudence, the promptings of humanity, alike demand that the war should be conducted with terrible energy—with that overmastering vigor which comes from the united efforts of a great people intent upon the vindication of the right. In this great national trial, reliance, under Providence, is upon the people. They need not only to be steadfast in their confidence of the justice of the cause, but *united* in its maintenance. May a generous enthusiasm for country animate all hearts, and the inspiration of a common purpose enable a firm and united people, with the pride of American citizens, to assert that, in spite of foes, domestic or foreign, " the great Republic " still lives, and shall survive as the rich legacy of the past and the hope of the future.

Very respecefully,
Your obedient servant,
LOT M. MORRILL.

Hon. JAMES W. WHITE, and others, *Committee.*

LETTER OF CHARLES SUMNER, SENATOR FROM MASSACHUSETTS.

SENATE CHAMBER, WASHINGTON, *July* 14*th*, 1862,

DEAR SIR :

I welcome and honor your patriotic efforts to arouse the country to a generous, determined, irresistible unity in support of our Government ; but the Senate is still in session, and my present post of duty is here. A senator cannot leave his post more than a soldier. But, absent or present, the cause in which the people are to assemble has my God speed—earnest, devoted, affectionate, from the heart. What I can do, let me do. There is no thing which I will not undertake, there is nothing which I will not renounce, if so I may serve my country. There must be unity of hands and of hearts, too, that the Republic may be lifted to the sublime idea of a true commonwealth, which, we are told, " ought to be as one huge Christian personage, one mighty growth and stature of an honest man, as big and compact in virtue as in body." Oh, sir, if my feeble voice could reach my fellow-countrymen in their workshops, in the streets, in the fields, and wherever they meet together ; if for one moment I could take to my lips that silver trumpet whose tones should sound and reverberate throughout the land, I would summon all, forgetting prejudice and turning away from error, to help unite, quicken and invigorate our common country—most beloved now that it is most imperiled—to a compactness and bigness of virtue in just proportion to its extended dominion, so that it should be as one huge Christian personage, one mighty growth and stature of an honest man, instinct with all the singleness of unity. Thus inspired, the gates of hell cannot prevail against us. To this end the cries of faction must be silenced, and the wickedness of sedition, whether in print or in public speech, must be suppressed. These are the Northern allies of the rebellion. An aroused and indignant people, with iron heel, ought to tread them out like the serpent, so that they can neither hiss nor sting. With such a concord God will be pleased, and he will fight for **us** ; he will give quickness to our armies, so that the hosts of the rebellion will be broken and scattered as by the thunderbolt; and he will give to our beneficent Government that blessed inspiration, better than any newly raised levies, by which the rebellion shall be struck in its single vulnerable part, by which that long cherished abomination which was its original mainspring and is its present motive power shall be overthrown; and by which the cause of the Union shall be linked with that Divine justice whose weapons are of celestial temper. God bless our country! and God bless all who now serve it with singleness of heart!

I have the honor to be, dear sir,
Your faithful servant,
CHARLES SUMNER.

LETTER OF M. F. ODELL, REPRESENTATIVE FROM NEW-YORK.

WASHINGTON, *July* 14*th*, 1862.

Charles Gould, Secretary, and others.

GENTLEMEN,—I am in receipt of your invitation to attend and address a mass meeting to be held to-morrow, the 15th inst., in New-York city.

It would be my pleasure to attend, but my duties here will prevent. You propose a gathering of men of all parties. Never, in my judgment, since the first rebel gun was fired, have there been reasons so strong as at this hour when all loyal and patriotic men should combine their energies to crush out, and put down forever, the foes of the Union. Whatever may have been our differences of opinion in relation to measures or policy, it must be evident to all good men, that this country can be saved and the Union maintained, by sustaining the government in its efforts to put down this rebellion. I have no doubt as to the results of this conflict. Our cause is just and right, and I believe there is a determination deep down in the hearts of the people to crush out this monster; hence I have confidence that men and means will be forthcoming as they are needed. I believe further, that it will be done with no compromises, until the last rebel shall ground his arms.

Yours, truly,
M. F. ODELL.

LETTER OF EDWARD HAIGHT, REPRESENTATIVE FROM NEW-YORK.

WASHINGTON CITY, *July* 14*th*, 1862.

Charles Gould, Esq., Sec'y of Select Committee, and others:

GENTLEMEN,—I am just in receipt of your invitation to attend a meeting of loyal citizens, on Tuesday next, and only regret that my duties here will prevent my being present in person. I most heartily, however, accord with the emphatic language of the call, and have no doubt, as to the hearty and cheerful response of the people to stop the *life-blood of the nation*, now rapidly flowing away.

The destiny and restoration of the Union is certain, and the opportunity to assist in its consummation, will be one, (if taken advantage of,) that will redound to the honor and credit of the participant for ages yet to come.

To preserve the Constitution and the Union, in their unity and integrity, to vindicate in *every part* of this Republic, one and indivisible, its supreme law, should be the paramount object of every loyal citizen.

Pledging untiring exertions to accomplish that end.

I am, gentlemen, very truly, yours,
EDWARD HAIGHT.
M. C. 9th Cong. Dist., N. Y.

LETTER OF ALFRED ELY, REPRESENTATIVE FROM NEW-YORK.

House of Representatives,
Washington, D. C., July 14th, 1862.

Charles Gould, Esq.:

Sir,—I duly received the letter addressed to me on the 11th instant, by a Committee of which you are Secretary, and which was constituted by the Common Council of New-York city, by the Chamber of Commerce of the State of New-York, by the Union Defence Committee, and by bodies of loyal citizens of New-York city, inviting me to address, to-morrow, a mass meeting in your city, of all parties who are in favor of supporting the Government in the prosecution of the war, and suppressing the rebellion.

I regret that my public duties will not allow me to accept this invitation. Congress is just upon the eve of an adjournment, and the transaction of the important business still before it, requires that a quorum of its members should remain here.

It would give me the greatest pleasure to be present to witness such an outpouring of the citizens of the commercial metropolis of the nation as I anticipate from their well-tried and unshaken loyalty, to testify " their undiminished confidence in the justice of the cause" in which we are engaged, and " their inflexible determination to sustain it." Such expressions as this mass meeting is designed to give, accompanied by the " proffer to the Government," by the people of the city of New-York, of " their aid to the extent of all their resources," will be of incalculable benefit to the country at home and abroad. It will silence faction among ourselves, and demonstrate to European powers that our front to the enemy is still solid and unbroken.

Begging you to accept for yourself and the Committee, and for their several constituencies, the assurances of my respect, I remain, sir, truly yours,
ALFRED ELY.

LETTER OF ROSCOE CONKLING, REPRESENTATIVE FROM NEW-YORK.

House of Representatives,
Washington, July 14th, 1862.

Gentlemen,—The duties resting upon a Representative in the closing hours of the present session, require me to be constantly in my seat. Were I at liberty to accept the invitation with which you have honored me, it would give me great pleasure to address a mass meeting of your citizens on Tuesday next.

Although debarred the privilege of participating in your proceedings, I shall regard them with an interest not likely ever again to attach to any similar occasion.

The exigencies and demands of the hour give to public action at this moment an importance which cannot now be realized. A great future is enshrouded in a little period immediately before us. The fate of our country depends upon the alacrity of its citizens. Your great metropolis has the leading part in the sacrifices, and the duties which await us.

The imperial position of our State was never shown so conspicuously: her resources and munificence have never been so indispensable to the whole nation, as since the outbreak of the present rebellion. The position New-York shall now assume will exert a commanding influence upon the final issue of our national difficulties, and the action of the meeting on Tuesday, will do much to awaken feeling throughout the State.

Let the city speak in emphatic tones in favor of sparing nothing that stands in the way of crushing treason at home, and repelling insolence from abroad. The meeting is timely, and I wish it complete success.

I have the honor to be, your obedient servant,
ROSCOE CONKLING.

Hon. James W. White, and others, *Committee.*

LETTER OF SCHUYLER COLFAX, REPRESENTATIVE FROM INDIANA.

House of Representatives,
Washington City, *July* 14th, 1862.

My Dear Sir:

I thank you for the honor conferred on me by the Committee of which you are Secretary, inviting me to address the meeting of the loyal citizens of my native city to-morrow, and assure you of my regret that public duties will prevent my attending. I doubt not that the Empire City will speak on that occasion in a manner and with an emphasis that will be heard and heeded throughout the entire Republic, as well as beyond the Atlantic; and that will prove that our country, doubly dear to us now, not only by the sacrifices of those who founded it, but by the more recent sacrifices of the brave soldiers who have defended it against traitors, is dearer to us all in its hour of trial than in its brightest era of peace and prosperity.

I cannot give you my opinion of the duty of this eventful hour in briefer terms than the following resolution, which I had the honor to offer at a largely attended Congressional caucus last Saturday evening, and which was adopted with gratifying unanimity:

"*Resolved*, That we hold it to be the duty of all loyal men to stand by the Union in this hour of its trial—to unite their hearts and hands in earnest and patriotic efforts for its maintenance against those who are in arms against it—to sustain, with determined resolution, our patriotic President and his administration in their most energetic efforts for the prosecution of the war and the preservation of the Union against enemies at home and abroad—to punish traitors and treason with fitting severity—and to so crush the present wicked and causeless rebellion that no flag of disunion shall ever again be raised over any portion of the Republic. That, to this end, we invite the co-operation of all men who love their country in the endeavor to rekindle throughout all the States such a patriotic fire as shall utterly consume all who strike at the Union of our Fathers, and all who sympathize with their treason or palliate their guilt."

Very truly, yours,
SCHUYLER COLFAX.

Chas. Gould, Esq., *Secretary, &c., &c.*

LETTER FROM COMMODORE ANDREW H. FOOTE.

New Haven, *July* 11th, 1862.

My Dear Sir:

Your kind letter, as a member of the committee on invitations and speakers at the mass meeting to be held in New-York, on Tuesday next, for the purpose of inciting a deeper interest in the public mind toward the prompt supply of men and means for crushing this atrocious rebellion, has been received.

I deeply regret that an imperative sense of duty to the Government, as well as to myself, prevents my complying with your invitation to be present and address the citizens of the great metropolis on such a momentous occasion. Still suffering from the effects of my wound received at Fort Donelson, although rapidly improving in health, my physicians have enjoined upon me the necessity of repose of mind and body for the present, as essential in enabling me to return at an early day to active service in the war.

We owe it to our honor as a nation, to our children and posterity, to transmit to them, if needs be with our blood and treasure, the preservation of the most free and beneficent government ever established upon the earth. Shall the North, with her twenty millions and untold resources, pusillanimously yield to six millions of miserable rebels in arms? No! death itself would be preferable to men who have any claim to manhood. Let every citizen, then, rush to the field, or furnish a substitute, to enable the heroic and accomplished leader of the Army of the Potomac, who is now awaiting reinforcements only, to strike the final blow in crushing forever this atrocious rebellion.

Let the ladies of New-York continue to give their support to this glorious cause. They are all potent in persuasive influence ; but in instances where this fails, let them decline—spurn—the attentions of all young men who remain at home when they might be in the fight vindicating the honor of our flag, until these young men shall present themselves as having done their part on the battle-field toward transmitting the rich legacy of such a Government as the indomitable courage of the fathers of our republic have bequeathed to their children.

Let the North but appreciate the crisis, and trusting in the God of battles, we will hurl defiance at our enemies, internal and external.

I am, respectfully, and very truly, yours,
ANDREW H. FOOTE.
Chas. Gould, Esq., New-York.

LETTER OF GEN. LEWIS WALLACE.

POUGHKEEPSIE, N. Y., *July* 17*th*, 1862.
Chas. Gould, Esq., Secretary, etc.

DEAR SIR,—The note from the Select Committee inviting me to address the meeting in your city on the 15th instant, has just reached me.

I regret it did not come in time to enable me to comply.

The army needs recruitment badly, and I am greatly pleased at the manner it is taken hold of in New-York.

Be kind enough to inform the committee why their favor was not sooner answered.   Very respectfully, sir,
Your friend and servant,
LEWIS WALLACE.

LETTER OF A. D. BACHE, SUPERINTENDENT OF UNITED STATES COAST SURVEY.

COAST SURVEY OFFICE,
WASHINGTON, D. C., *July* 14*th*, 1862.
GENTLEMEN :

I thank you cordially for the opportunity you give me of being present at the meeting of "loyal citizens," on Tuesday, the 15th instant. Every one of your watchwords touch the very depths of my heart. No party, but the whole country. A union of all for the support of the Government in an energetic prosecution of the war for the suppression of the rebellion. Undiminished confidence in the justice of the cause. Inflexible determination to sustain it. Aid to the Government to the extent of all resources of mind, body and estate. How must such words stir the souls of all loyal citizens ! How much I regret that I may not, consistently with pressing duties, enjoy the enthusiasm of this mass meeting.

The corps to which I belong is dispersed among the army and navy expeditions in Virginia, North and South Carolina, Florida and Louisiana, lending the aid of their minute local knowledge freely to the army and navy expeditions. After this service they will be ready to continue maps of the coast and to contribute personal information which will be useful in case of intervention, as that already contributed has been against rebellion. All these men would be delighted to be counted as particles in the mass meeting of loyal citizens. All unite with me in three times three cheers for the watchwords of your committee.

Very respectfully yours,
A. D. BACHE.
JAMES W. WHITE, GEORGE OPDYKE, SAMUEL SLOAN, PROSPER M. WETMORE, DENNING DUER, CHARLES GOULD, *Select Committee.*

LETTER FROM REV. H. W. BELLOWS, PRESIDENT OF SANITARY COMMISSION.

WASHINGTON, D. C., July 12th, 1862.

J. W. White, Geo. Opdyke, &c.

GENTLEMEN,—I regret that my previous engagements, which carry me to another section of our troubled country, will not permit me to accept your invitation to address the people of New-York at the mass meeting of loyal citizens on the 15th instant. I should rejoice to participate in that important meeting. The *masses* are the great constituents of those who are waging this defence of democratic institutions against the assaults of the proudest aristocracy in the world. It is not slavery, but the aristocratic spirit of feudalism, which simply finds its accidental expression in negro slavery, which is now making its last and most bloody struggle (in modern history) in this civil war. We are fighting the poor man's, the working-man's, the foreign emigrant's, the mechanic's, the clerk's battle. Their *last* battle for political and social equality. Feudalism on the other side of the water, in all her various shapes—French, English, and Austrian—hates our prospect of success, and loves every rebel who strikes us with bullet or bayonet, as if he were in her own employ. But, if we have the aristocrats of the whole world against us, we have *the people* of the whole world with us! We are fighting against thrones and principalities and powers—fighting for equal rights, the poor man's liberties, the dignity of labor, and the principle of self-government. We are fighting for the gospel of Christ, in its political expression, against the religions of caste and the hierarchies of birth and blood. When the people *know* this, every man will drop his quill, his last, his spade, his hammer his hod, his ledger, his comfort, his party prejudices, his home and his fortune, to enlist! That is the thing to do, and to do at once. It is the only practical proof of patriotism that ought to be accepted from an able-bodied man, between twenty and forty, at this crisis of liberty and democratic existence.

Yours, with utmost sympathy,
H. W. BELLOWS.

LETTER OF EDWARD EVERETT.

BOSTON, 14th July, 1862.

Charles Gould, Esq.:

DEAR SIR,—I received, a moment since, a copy of your circular of the 11th, inviting me to attend a mass meeting of loyal citizens, of all parties, in New-York, to-morrow. It would give me great pleasure, if it were in my power, to take part in a meeting, called in the great Metropolis of the Union, for the patriotic purposes indicated in the circular; but my official duty as a member of the Board of Overseers of Harvard College, requires me to be at Cambridge on Commencement day, the 16th.

New-York needs no voice from abroad to cheer her in the path of duty, at this momentous crisis.

I remain, dear sir, very respectfully, yours,
EDWARD EVERETT.

LETTER OF JOHN A KING.

JAMAICA, L. I., July 14th, 1862.

Charles Gould, Esq., Secretary of Committee of Loyal Citizens:

DEAR SIR,—I beg to acknowledge and thank you for the invitation to address the meeting of loyal citizens, to-morrow afternoon, in the city of New-York. Concurring fully in the patriotic object and purposes of the meeting, I hope to be present on the occasion, but must ask to be excused from taking an active part in the proceedings of the meeting.

With great respect, your obedient servant,
JOHN A KING.

LETTER OF LYMAN TREMAIN.

ALBANY, *July* 14*th*, 1862.

GENT. :

I am in receipt of your invitation to ad'.ess the mass meeting to be held on the 15th instant.

It gives me great pleasure to learn that such a meeting is called. I trust it will be worthy of the great city where it will be held, worthy of the occasion, and of the noble cause in whose service it will be convened.

I regret to say that an engagement to address a similar meeting in this city, the same evening, will put it beyond my power to attend.

Yours truly,
LYMAN TREMAIN.

CHAS. GOULD, Esq , *Sec. &c.*

LETTER OF WM. M. EVARTS.

WINDSOR, VT., *July* 15*th*, 1862.

DEAR SIR:

The invitation of your committee to address the great meeting, to be held to-day, in the city of New-York, reached me too late for this answer, even, to be in time for the occasion.

The enthusiastic rally at Union Square, on the twentieth of April of last year, demonstrated the wisdom and courage of our people in instantly meeting the war, which had been opened against the Government by the armed rebellion, with all the strength and energy which thorough and united purpose and abundant material resources cou'd supply. From that moment the people have taken no step backward, and there has been more occasion for solicitude that they would run over the Government than that they would not keep up with its movements and demands. I have no fears now, that the response of the people to the new call for troops, will be either sluggish or inadequate.

Whether in the past, the Government has fully understood the stern simplicity of this contest—to which only two issues, the destruction of its enemy or of itself, were ever possible; whether it has recognized its true enemy—the rebel aristocracy—and appreciated the depth and force of the passions and interests which have stimulated their hatred and support their hostilities ; whether it has wisely and effectively employed the immense power which the devotion of the people has laid at its feet ;—these are questions unsuited to the situation of our affairs. " Forgetting the things that are behind " we " must press forward," and be satisfied with knowing and insisting that, in the future, the sentiments and action of the Government will be, and shall be, clear, decisive and concentrated ; seeking, what thus seeking it is sure to accomplish, the rapid and complete reduction, by military power, of the revolted territory and population to allegiance to their and our Constitution.

I know that there are loyal, intelligent and earnest lovers of their country, who conceive that they have no part or heart in this war, if it be not so directed that the social institution of s'avery shall not survive it, and others who imagine that they will not help put down the rebellion if slavery is to fall with it. But these opinions *govern* no considerable number of the loyal population : and, indeed, if those who profess the one or the other of them, were put to the test, I am persuaded that the Flag and the Constitution would lose few of them as defenders.

And now it is proclaimed, as with a trumpet, throughout the land, to rebels and to loyal men alike, that the burden and the heat of the war are upon us ; that our manhood and our birthright are in the issue ; and that the sun which sets upon this day of our trial, will look upon us a proud, a happy, a free, a powerful nation, or a rent, distracted, crushed, despised people.

How foolish and feeble a conception of the fates that this war carries, have they, who regard it as a contest involving, only, the extent of territory and of population which our Government shall maintain dominion over. A mutilated territory and a dismembered people are results sufficiently intolerable to our pride and our interests. But the disastrous event of this war stops at no such measure of calamity. The Federal Constitution itself will have been rent in twain, and the fabric of our National liberties will have passed away as a scroll. The noble heritage which the wisdom and courage of heroic ancestors gained for us will have been wrested from our feeble and faithless hands. For this, our self-abasement, there will be "no cure, no after-health, no pardon."

I believe that the people understand this momentous issue, and that their hearts thrill with the intensity of the emotions its contemplation begets. Have we, by Divine favor, the *power* to avert this ruin and maintain the life of the Nation? This power can be none other than military and financial resources, and the wisdom and courage to apply them.

The mass of the population supporting the Government, and counting as the supply of its military and financial strength, numbers about twenty-three millions, of which something like a million are slaves. The mass of the population arrayed in revolt is over eight millions, of which three millions are slaves. We thus stand four to one of the free population of the country, for the Government. Are these five millions of free whites, mounted on the shoulders of three million black slaves, able to predominate over our twenty millions of free whites, in battle and in war, as they have done in politics and in peace? If they are, they had better be *dismounted*.

But the question carries its own answer. If, on our part, the battles are still political, and the war peaceful, this treason will overthrow our Government. If we are to save the lives, the property, the feelings and the pride of the rebels, and waste only the lives, the courage and the strength of the loyal people, we are the *allies* of the rebels, not their enemies, and undermine, from within, the citadel, which they assault from without.

If, on the other hand, we will dismiss politics and peace from our minds and from our hearts; if our advancing armies shall treat the population in revolt. whether black or white, slave or free, as *war groups* them—as rebel or as loyal, as hostile or as submissive; if the Government will execute the simple policy, " *parcere subjectis, debellare superbos*,"—root out the haughty aristocracy that urges on the rebellion, and spare the abject followers it has cheated and forced into its support, "the hand of the Government will be in the neck of its enemies." We shall see this treason crouch and cower under the thunderbolts of war, and the leaders of the revolt strangled in the cruel rage with which the terrified and suffering masses will seek for victims, to save themselves and make peace with the Government.

Thus far the weakness of our sentiments has been the strength of the rebellion. The battles of the Peninsula—so glorious to our soldiery—have made any further feebleness of purpose, or random aim, impossible, but at the cost of the nation's life. The Government and the people are now thoroughly aroused, thoroughly informed. Our rulers will lead, and we shall follow, fast and far. Everything is full of courage and strength, and the tide of WAR will never ebb till we are, again, one people, with one Constitution and one destiny.

I cannot be at your meeting, but in the earnest and patriotic activity which will there receive new impulse, I shall give every aid of time, of money, and of labor which shall be in my power.

I am, with great respect to yourself and the Committee,

Your obedient servant,

WM. M. EVARTS.

To CHAS. GOULD, Esq., *Secretary, &c.*

LETTER OF JAMES T. BRADY.

NEW-YORK, *July 15th*, 1862.

Hon. George Opdyke:

DEAR SIR,—I regret that I will not be able to address my fellow-citizens at the Union Meeting called for this afternoon, being troubled with an affection of the throat, which prevents my making such an effort as would be required to speak before a large assemblage, in the open air.

I am sorry that some of our countrymen are so prone to despond or complain, because we do not triumph in every encounter with our opponents, and that the appreciation of great victories in the past, is lost in mourning over the discomfitures of the hour.

It is quite likely that errors have been committed in the conduct of the present war. By whom, when, and how, will all be certainly made known hereafter. We have no time now for lamentations or complaints. The whole of our thoughts and efforts should be applied in vigorously devoting the power of the present, so as to secure prosperity in the future. We are engaged in a war with men who display a fierce resolution to overcome us by force of arms. If we do not defeat them, they will defeat us. Our course is, therefore, very plain. We should cheerfully and energetically sustain the Government in putting down the rebellion, and restoring our national authority. For this purpose more men are required. They must and will be furnished. No fear of consequences, such as might offend our political opinions, should for one moment obstruct this exhibition of loyalty. We did not invite nor begin the war. We sought to prevent a calamity so dire. It is the work of ambitious and bad leaders at the South, whose defeat and disgrace will surely come. When we succeed, as we ultimately shall, then, and not before, will be the time to decide upon all the grave political questions which may arise out of the conflict now progressing, or the cause which produced it. The supremacy of our laws is indispensable to ensure a full and free discussion of those questions at the South. It is quite obvious that we must have more troops, not only to meet the present exigencies, but also to provide for those which may hereafter arise. It is well to prepare for foreign intervention, although I see little cause for apprehending such an occurrence. France is not in a condition to neglect her own affairs, and attend to ours. England has not for many years shown much eagerness to engage in hostilities with a formidable power. I am loth to believe that any large number of the English people will be found as malignant, false, or vacillating as the London *Times*. If intervention by a foreign government is ever to happen, I wish it would occur now, while our people have their military spirit aroused. Such a wicked assault upon us would call into the field every man on our soil who was capable of bearing arms. And it is not likely that if France, for the first time, appeared as our enemy, in a foul alliance with Britain, the continent would look on with entire indifference, and furnish us no aid against ancient enemies. Let us have an army under whose protection we can safely and decently announce, that while we seek no quarrel with any nation, neither will we avoid one, when to do so would, in the slightest degree, impair our strength, prosperity, or honor.

For my own part, I have confidence in the intelligence, patriotism and judgment of the President and his cabinet, although in saying this I do not mean to assert that the course adopted by him or them has, in every instance, been the wisest or best for the occasion. I have confidence in General McClellan. I know that, however foes or slanderers may assail him, he has, and will have, to sustain him in every event, the gratitude, admiration, and love of the masses. Time will confirm this statement, if there be now one reason to discredit it.

I have no doubt, whatever, that we are to win the fight in which we are engaged. It may be protracted; it may involve unparalleled outlay of treasure, loss of life, and suffering. But, dreadful as these consequences are, we must encounter them all to preserve the republic, keep unsullied the honor of our flag, and prevent the coming of a time when it may truly be said that there is no such power on earth as "The United States of America."

We are solving the great problem whether a free government, founded on the free action of the people, can be permanently maintained. In the solution of that question, it is not alone the American people, or this generation, that is interested. It deeply concerns the whole world. It is to affect the happiness of races and generations to come. That is one reason why the natives of so many lands nobly unite with the American, in the struggle for our success. Let all who feel a desire that we should triumph, forget everything else in the enthusiastic endeavor to make that triumph certain.

Yours, truly,

JAMES T. BRADY.

LETTER OF RICHARD BUSTEED, ESQ.

NEW-YORK, July 12th, 1862,
237 BROADWAY.

Hon. James W. White, Geo. Opdyke, Samuel Sloan, Prosper M. Wetmore, Denning Duer, Charles Gould, Select Committee, &c.:

GENTLEMEN,—I regret it is not in my power to accept your invitation to address the mass meeting to be held in this city on the 15th inst. Circumstances wholly beyond my control, will prevent me the pleasure I would derive from being present to swell the chorus of patriotism which on that day will arise from the great heart of loyal New-York, in support of the Government, and in unmistakable rebuke of treason and traitors at home, and maligners and meddlers abroad.

Be assured, gentlemen, of my entire sympathy in the movement. I regard it as a step in the right direction, and rejoice that there is among our people, an "inflexible determination to sustain" the Government, without reference to mere political views, and looking only to the re-establishment of its power over every acre of its soil, and every one of its subjects.

The time is when party must be lost sight of in the higher claims of duty and fealty to country. Who falters now in these, let him henceforward be distrusted, let his name be a byword and a scorn, let him live in shame and die in dishonor. Let it be understood and declared that,

<blockquote>
"Freedom's soil has only place
For a free and fearless race;
None for traitors false and base."
</blockquote>

In this terrible struggle for life, we must not fail. Our shortcoming would justly be accounted treason to the race, and impiety to God. We cannot fail but by being false to the commonest instincts of honor and pride. Let no true man carp now. No real patriot will retard the success of our cause either by personal supineness, or by indulging in criticisms upon the Government, which have the effect of antagonisms. Let it be left to our enemies to cavil, while we bear proudly aloft, and hold up to the wistful gaze of the world, the standard of Constitutional Freedom, symbolized by an unimpaired American nationality.

With great respect,

Your fellow-citizen,
RICHARD BUSTEED.

LETTER OF REV. J. P. THOMPSON.

No. 32 WEST THIRTY-SIXTH STREET, }
July 14th, 4 P. M., 1862.

DEAR SIR:

The invitation of the Select Committee of the Chamber of Commerce, to address the mass meeting at Union Square, to-morrow, has just come to hand. Most gladly would I contribute in any way to the object of that meeting—the support of the Government in suppressing the rebellion—an object to which I am ready to devote time, means, labor, children, whatever I possess or can influence for so great a cause. All that is dear to us for ourselves and our children, all that is dear to us as friends of freedom and of humanity, all that is dear to us as Christians, seeking to establish and to perfect upon this western continent a civilization founded upon public virtue and equity, the fear of God and the rights of man; all of value from the past, of good in the present, of hope for the future—demands that this atrocious rebellion be subdued, and its more atrocious cause be utterly exterminated.

Yours truly,

JOS. P. THOMPSON.

CHAS. GOULD. Esq.

LETTER OF GEORGE GIBBS, OF WASHINGTON TERRITORY.

WASHINGTON CITY, July 13th, 1862.

SIR:

I have the honor to acknowledge the receipt of your invitation to address the mass meeting of loyal citizens in Union Square, New-York, on 15th inst. I regret that official business prevents my accepting the call. Let me assure you, however, that though no one may officially represent the Territory of Washington at the contemplated meeting, I can answer for the truth and fidelity of her people to the Union, without question and without qualification.

I am sir, very truly,

Your obedient servant,

GEORGE GIBBS.

CHARLES GOULD, Esq., *Secretary.*

OPINIONS OF THE PRESS.

[*From the New-York World, July 16th.*]

The grand demonstration at Union Square, yesterday afternoon, was a gathering in every way worthy of the great cause that had called it forth. An hour previous to the time named for the meeting, the Park was crowded with men and women anxious to secure eligible positions, where they could sit in the shade and listen to the music for the Union.

From the hotels and housetops, and from the churches, the stars and stripes were displayed with the utmost profusion. The windows looking from the residences upon all sides of the Square were thrown up, and the balconies fronting them filled with ladies and children, whose presence served greatly to add to the animation of the scene below. Broadway and the other thoroughfares leading to the Square were thronged with the multitudes who had closed their stores and workshops to attend the meeting. Every class and trade were represented. The wealthy millionaire, who had left the luxuries of a well-filled table and dashed up in a splendid equipage, had come prepared to counsel with the hard-fisted laborer who had left mattock and spade, crow-bar and barrow, to devise means for maintaining the Union; and the voices of both were unanimous that "it must and shall be preserved."

The stands were ranged in numerical order, beginning with No. 1, at the monument, passing round the Square in a north-westerly direction, and terminating with No. 5. They were substantial structures, and beautifully draped with bunting, the stars and stripes being conspicuous over all. Around these the crowd began to assemble at half-past three o'clock; and from that moment the numbers increased until the hour of adjournment. The utmost enthusiasm prevailed upon all sides. Bands of music were playing at intervals, and Anthon's Light Battery boomed forth a welcome to the coming thousands who were marshaling from town and country in a common cause. As the gathering grew more dense, the cars on the Fourth Avenue Railroad ceased running—it being impossible for them to get through. The Broadway stages ran off their line also, the entire space occupied by the Square being given up unreservedly to the purposes of the meeting. Prominent in the assemblage were the veterans of the war of 1812, in uniform, their swords buckled on as if ready for another contest, and their voices urging the young men everywhere to enlist.

At four o'clock the workingmen from the lower wards came up *en masse*, and shortly afterward the "jackets of blue" from the Navy Yard made their appearance; also the ship-carpenters at work on the Union gun-boats, the workmen from Singer's sewing-machine manufactory, and those employed by Henry Brewster & Co.; these latter assisting to work the Anthon Battery.

The New England Soldiers' Relief Association had two huge wagons, one drawn by eight horses and the other by four horses, covered with flags, both laden with patriotic hearts, anxious with the rest to help on the great cause of crushing the rebellion.

It was a mass meeting in every sense of the word. The presence of 100,000 men stamped it as earnest, and likely to be productive of untold results. It was a mass meeting in point of numbers, of wealth, of class, of respectability, and, above all, of loyalty and devotion to the grand old Union. Even the boys in the street paraded in uniform, waving the American flag, and cheering the patriotic utterances of their elders. Looking from the several stands, the eye encountered a sea of faces not commonly met at great gatherings. There was an almost utter absence of levity and disorder. Every countenance said plainly that its owner had come there with an earnest purpose; that the time for trifling had passed; that the great crisis was at hand; and, by the help of God and their own right arms, that they meant to meet the issue as became American freemen, worthy to preserve the liberties transmitted them by their fathers.

[*From the Evening Post, July 16th.*]

If the great meeting of April, 1861, was more numerous and enthusiastic than that of yesterday, it was because the nation then felt the first glow of its patriotic ardor. But, with the exception of that grand outbreak, no meeting ever held in the city has surpassed the one of yesterday in grandeur and life. A sea of men and women filled the vast spaces around Union Square, so that streets, sidewalks, balconies and windows were filled, while the proceedings were marked throughout by the utmost animation. In the eloquent speeches of General Walbridge, Judge Daly, Dr. Hitchcock, Mr. Coddington, Delafield Smith, and others, there was a noble utterance of the grand pervading sentiment of the occasion.

We have given elsewhere such reports of the speeches and doings as our space admits, and we design in this column merely to record impressions produced upon us by a careful observation of the masses assembled. The war impulse is apparently as vigorous and determined as it ever was; the devotion of the people to the Union is as strong; but this patriotic zeal is tempered by a greater thoughtfulness. A year ago we were ready to rush into battle without preparation, and despising the enemy like a troop of headlong boys, who love excitement and are reckless of consequences. But at this time, though we are no less determined to fight, we desire to do so with a distinct object and a careful estimate of the means. We have learned from experience that our enemy, being of our own blood, is no despicable opponent; we know his desperation; and we feel that he is only to be overcome by the most strenuous and persistent efforts. We cannot play with him any longer, and if we fight him we must fight him in grim and deadly earnest. We must not stand on trifles if we mean to put down the rebellion speedily and forever.

The single result of this great assemblage has been to express the necessity of a more active and stringent prosecution of hostilities. No other opinion was uttered; no other sentiment tolerated. A drunken fellow near Fremont's stand began to mutter something about "abolitionists," but he was instantly silenced by the cry that the war must go on at all hazards, and by every means in our power. No one tries to revive those old partisan cries who is not in the interest of secession, while loyal men and women everywhere will echo the resolve of this gigantic congregation, to urge " upon the Government the exercise of its utmost skill and vigor in the prosecution of this war, unity of design, comprehensiveness of plan, a uniform policy and a stringent use of all the means within its reach, consistent with the usages of civilized warfare."

[*From the Commercial Advertiser, July 16.*]

The gathering of the loyal people of this city at Union Square, yesterday afternoon, exceeded the expectations of the most sanguine. In numbers, character and exalted patriotism, it has had no parallel on this continent. The sight of the congregated thousands was calculated to make a New-Yorker feel proud of his citizenship. The unanimity of sentiment was marvelous. One loyal pulse beat through the whole mass. One foolish man, apparently of foreign birth, paraded the crowd with a white pocket-kerchief attached to a walking cane, and could not conceal his mortification that he was met everywhere by a smile of contempt. At length, however, somebody gave him a hint that he had made a fool of himself long enough, and he was glad of an excuse to "skedaddle." We have said that the unanimity of the multitudinous gathering was marvelous, and we may add that the universal sentiment was that the Federal Government should be supported in the extremest measures that might be deemed necessary for speedily as well as effectually putting down the infamous revolt of the Southern States.

One naturally connects the meeting of yesterday with the great Union meeting held in the same place when first the news was received that the rebels of Charleston had commenced war against the United States by their attack upon Fort Sumter and its feeble garrison. In some respects there was a similarity between the two meetings, but in other respects a material difference. That of yesterday was much the larger, as we affirm on personal observation. This was scarcely to be anticipated, considering what liberal contributions the Empire City has made to the Federal army. The fact, however, is suggestive. In the former meeting a universal excitement had suddenly seized upon the community, and every man who loved his country felt all the maddening anguish of the insult offered to its flag, without any realization of the sacrifice that would have to be made before that insult could be properly resented and punished. Yesterday loyal men came together, after having not only counted the cost of vindicating the country's honor, but having themselves in their persons, their property or their families, actually borne a share of such sacrifice. And yet were the people yesterday even more determined and enthusiastic in their patriotism and devotion to the Union than were those in April last.

Nor can we withhold our testimony respecting another important feature of yesterday's meeting. That vast multitude most unmistakably declared themselves in favor of increased vigor in the prosecution of the war, and of greater severity of treatment to those in arms against the Federal Government. And the speakers were manifestly of the same mind. All felt and said that lenity was thrown away upon the vindictive men who have sought, for their own aggrandizement, the severance of this glorious Union. Men heretofore proverbial for their conservatism--public men who have in days past counseled the exhaustion of all conciliatory measures that could be employed without sacrifice of dignity and right on the part of the Federal Government—merchants whose commercial connection with the South has not unnaturally rendered them averse to extreme measures against the rebels,—prominent politicians, whose party sympathies and party hopes have been bound up with the South--all yesterday agreed and emphatically declared that the Government must no longer hesitate to employ every power, the use of which is authorized by the laws of warfare, to put a speedy and perpetual end to the rebellion ; and the more emphatically this purpose was declared the more enthusiastic was the applause.

Another gratifying feature of the meeting was that every allusion to the necessity of further enlistments in the Federal army met with a no less enthusiastic response, while the living mass that filled the Square told plainly that this city has the material for more than its proportion of the additional forces called for. No one who saw the meeting of last night and heard the yearnings and the outbursts of its patriotism can for a moment entertain any apprehension that volunteers will be lacking to bear the banner of the Union victoriously to the extremest point of its Southern territory. We should have rejoiced greatly could the President of the United States have seen and heard what transpired in Union Park Square yesterday. He would have received a vivid and indelible impression of this truth, that if he will but strike the rebellion heavily, promptly, decisively, a popular support will go with him that will be irresistible.

[*From the New-York Times, July 16th.*]

THE VOICE OF THE METROPOLIS.—The great popular demonstration in this city, yesterday, was of a spirit and character sufficiently decided and enthusiastic. It, with the April demonstration of last year, forms the second of the two largest and most influential meetings ever held in New-York. It proclaimed, in unmistakable language and in clear voice, the purpose of the people in regard to the war and in support of the Union and the Government. From every stand and by every speaker there was but one tone; and every man present seemed inspired by the spirit of the hour. It was that the war begun by traitors must be pushed on till treason is extirpated from the whole land; that the Union which, during the year has cost so much blood and treasure, must be battled for while any blood or treasure is left in the country; and that, to this end, the legitimate directors of the war must be upheld in every effort for its successful prosecution, and impelled onward by the people to greater efforts and the most decisive measures. Though during the year thousands of the bravest and best of the sons of New-York have given their lives for the sacred cause, there were yet thousands more ready to meet the ordeal of battle for its support; and though tens of thousands were now on the battle-field in Virginia, there would be no lack of men willing to follow them there or anywhere else. They were in favor of the *strongest measures* on the part of the Government: the most determined vigor on the part of commanders; the most unflinching prosecution of the war. The most energetic words were applauded with most vehemence; the most courageous expressions met with the warmest response in the people's hearts. There was no talk of discouragement, not the shadow of a thought of doubt of ultimate triumphant success. Recent disasters were acknowledged and felt to be but temporary and accidental; and the long roll of victories that glorify the year gave faith that the triumphs of our arms in the future would be none the less prouder and decisive.

There could not have been greater *unanimity* displayed on the part of all classes and parties in New-York. Men of every political antecedent and of every social grade agreed and fraternized, as they have done in the past. There was no thought of any sort of compromise—not a man who dared to propose to turn the back toward the enemy. All felt that whatever stood in the nation's pathway must be broken through, and that nothing in the South nor in the North was so sacred as the Unity of the Republic. On this point the voice of the people, as expressed yesterday, was unmistakable.

The meeting of April, last year, was held the day after our troops had been assaulted in Baltimore, and the first blood had been shed in the war. It gave an impetus to volunteering and to the National cause throughout the whole country; it gave strength and vigor to the Administration, consolidated the sentiment of the city, and was the first unmistakable evidence of a united North. The North has remained united throughout the year, and its unity is still unbroken; and to this fact, next to the courage of our army, is owing the triumphs of the past over the rebellion. This meeting gives a further expression to the same purpose of the North; and if it does as much to stimulate the country and aid the Government, it will be a success.

New-York now has had its day of talk. The next work in hand is *fighting*. The people have spoken; now let them buckle on the armor. There is spirit enough, courage enough, faith enough; let there be no backwardness in volunteering. Three hundred thousand troops are needed—needed at once. Our gallant army, which marched to the field a year ago, has already done more than half the work of crushing the rebellion, and restoring the Union. The men required to aid in finishing the other half of the labor must hasten to do it, and put the capstone of restoration on the National temple. If the masses of the Metropolis act up promptly to the spirit they evinced yesterday, our quota of troops will be in the field before the close of the week.

[*From the New-York Herald, July 16.*]

THE CRISIS.—THE VOICE OF NEW-YORK.—NO SACRIFICE TOO GREAT FOR THE UNION.—The city of New-York, *en masse*, has risen and spoken again for the Union. Yesterday, in Union Square, we had a re-enactment of the sublime spectacle of April, 1861, and a reaffirmation of the same patriotic spirit and determination of our loyal citizens—everything for the Union.

Our great day of April, a year ago, was the response of New-York city to the President's primary call for seventy-five thousand men to maintain " the integrity of the Union," violently assailed by a rebellious conspiracy in the bombardment of Fort Sumter ; and that indignant uprising of New-York rallied the loyal North, like the call of a trumpet, to the support of the President. This second grand council of our citizens, after fifteen months of war by land and sea, and after the contribution by our city and State to our army and navy of not less than one hundred and twenty-five thousand men, is in answer to another call of the President for reinforcements to our army to the extent of three hundred thousand men. Anticipating, too, from the diffusion of this imposing demonstration, such an awakening of our loyal States and people as will meet all the demands of this crisis, we devote a large portion of our available space to-day to the productions of this grand assemblage, in order to spread them broadcast over the land, and to the encouragement of the friends of our great cause and the terror of its enemies at home and abroad.

The address of this meeting and the accompanying resolutions speak authoritatively the voice of our loyal citizens. They stand upon the solid platform of President Lincoln—"The integrity of the Union"—its supremacy, and our Federal Constitution. They expose the disorganizing and anarchical elements of this Southern rebellion with peculiar force—its absurd and hypocritical pretences, and its demoralizing and destructive tendencies. The address in question, after fully establishing the legal supremacy of the Union and its political necessities, condenses the argument into the simple impressive facts that we are fighting · for the integrity of our country, for our national existence, for the Christian civilization of our land, for our commerce, our arts, our schools : for all those earthly things which we have been taught most to cherish and respect."

The war, then, on our part, is to be prosecuted to the extent of our men. means and resources, for the suppression of this rebellion : and against any hostile foreign intervention whatever, the Government can count on the unanimous support of our loyal States and people. Such is the spirit of the address adopted by the city of New-York at this mass meeting, and the accompanying resolutions are equally emphatic in defining our position. The city of New-York looks to no alternative but the suppression of this rebellion. She stands by our gallant armies in the field ; she is prepared for any sacrifice to reinforce and strengthen them ; she approves the wise, just and consistent Union war policy of President Lincoln ; she urges the Government to " lose no time in filling up our armies and putting the whole sea-coast in a state of complete deferee," and she knows no such word as fail.

Each of the numerous speakers on the occasion, though differing from the rest more or less, supports this paramount idea of the vigorous prosecution of the war. We submit our copious reports to the careful attention of our readers ; and for their more complete information in regard to the late and the present position of General McClellan's army, in this connection, we give them a very interesting illustrative map of the field of war around the city of Richmond. New-York city has spoken, and while the country is responding to her cheering voice let us proceed to action. Let us set an example in action by a prompt contribution of twenty thousand fresh soldiers to our armies in Virginia. That number we ought to be able to draw from this grand mass meeting in Union Square.

[*From the New-York Tribune, July 16.*]

NEW-YORK IS CONSTANT.—A year ago last April, our city held what was probably the largest public meeting ever convened in America, to emphasize her determination to stand firmly and fully by the Federal Government, in the struggle just forced upon it by the slaveholding traitors, in devoting her last dollar and musket to the maintenance of the Union, and the support of its fairly chosen and rightful authorities. That meeting was unequaled in numbers, in unanimity and in dauntless resolution.

Nearly fifteen months have since passed, and again our city has mustered her tens of thousands to attest anew her devotion to the country and her cause. If the first flush of enthusiasm has passed away, it has been succeeded by a graver, and sterner, more inflexible resolution. At the former meeting, the hope was still cherished that the traitor chiefs would be left to their own devices, and that the Southern masses would compel their assent to a speedy and bloodless reunion. That hope has been dissipated. Though the original and determined secessionists were less than one hundred thousand in number, they have managed to bully or awe the great body of the southern whites into subserviency to their treason. Only from the despised, oppressed, calumniated human chattels of these rebels, has the Union cause any hope of defenders in the States given over to the machinations of traitors.

The meeting of yesterday was a fresh exhibition of the earnestness and unanimity wherewith the Union is cherished in the hearts and hopes of our citizens. But it was more than this—it was an entreaty, an exhortation to the Government to employ every influence, every instrument, every energy, in putting down the slaveholders' rebellion.

www.ingramcontent.com/pod-product-compliance
Lightning Source LLC
Chambersburg PA
CBHW020136170426
43199CB00010B/767